Goal Digger Journal
for Essential Oil Business Builders

by Jennifer Wallner

JANUARY

JANUARY 1ST

☐ Supplements   ☐ Water   ☐ Meditate/Mindset   ☐ Movement

To Do List:

☐ _____

☐ _____

☐ _____

☐ _____

☐ _____

New Prospect Contacts:

☐ _____

☐ _____

Follow-Up Contacts:

☐ _____

☐ _____

Customer Contacts:

☐ _____

☐ _____

Builder Contacts:

☐ _____

☐ _____

Gratitude:

☐ _____

JANUARY 2ND

□ Supplements   □ Water   □ Meditate/Mindset   □ Movement

To Do List:

- □ _____
- □ _____
- □ _____
- □ _____
- □ _____

New Prospect Contacts:

- □ _____
- □ _____

Follow-Up Contacts:

- □ _____
- □ _____

Customer Contacts:

- □ _____
- □ _____

Builder Contacts:

- □ _____
- □ _____

Gratitude:

- □ _____

JANUARY 3RD

☐ Supplements   ☐ Water   ☐ Meditate/Mindset   ☐ Movement

To Do List:

☐ _____

☐ _____

☐ _____

☐ _____

☐ _____

New Prospect Contacts:

☐ _____

☐ _____

Follow-Up Contacts:

☐ _____

☐ _____

Customer Contacts:

☐ _____

☐ _____

Builder Contacts:

☐ _____

☐ _____

Gratitude:

☐ _____

JANUARY 4TH

☐ Supplements   ☐ Water   ☐ Meditate/Mindset   ☐ Movement

To Do List:

☐ _____

☐ _____

☐ _____

☐ _____

☐ _____

New Prospect Contacts:

☐ _____

☐ _____

Follow-Up Contacts:

☐ _____

☐ _____

Customer Contacts:

☐ _____

☐ _____

Builder Contacts:

☐ _____

☐ _____

Gratitude:

☐ _____

JANUARY 5TH

□ Supplements   □ Water   □ Meditate/Mindset   □ Movement

To Do List:

□ _____

□ _____

□ _____

□ _____

□ _____

New Prospect Contacts:

□ _____

□ _____

Follow-Up Contacts:

□ _____

□ _____

Customer Contacts:

□ _____

□ _____

Builder Contacts:

□ _____

□ _____

Gratitude:

□ _____

JANUARY 6TH

☐ Supplements   ☐ Water   ☐ Meditate/Mindset   ☐ Movement

To Do List:

☐ _____
☐ _____
☐ _____
☐ _____
☐ _____

New Prospect Contacts:

☐ _____
☐ _____

Follow-Up Contacts:

☐ _____
☐ _____

Customer Contacts:

☐ _____
☐ _____

Builder Contacts:

☐ _____
☐ _____

Gratitude:

☐ _____

JANUARY 7TH

☐ Supplements   ☐ Water   ☐ Meditate/Mindset   ☐ Movement

To Do List:

☐ _____

☐ _____

☐ _____

☐ _____

☐ _____

New Prospect Contacts:

☐ _____

☐ _____

Follow-Up Contacts:

☐ _____

☐ _____

Customer Contacts:

☐ _____

☐ _____

Builder Contacts:

☐ _____

☐ _____

Gratitude:

☐ _____

JANUARY 8TH

□ Supplements   □ Water   □ Meditate/Mindset   □ Movement

To Do List:

□ _____

□ _____

□ _____

□ _____

□ _____

New Prospect Contacts:

□ _____

□ _____

Follow-Up Contacts:

□ _____

□ _____

Customer Contacts:

□ _____

□ _____

Builder Contacts:

□ _____

□ _____

Gratitude:

□ _____

JANUARY 9TH

□ Supplements   □ Water   □ Meditate/Mindset   □ Movement

To Do List:

□ _____

□ _____

□ _____

□ _____

□ _____

New Prospect Contacts:

□ _____

□ _____

Follow-Up Contacts:

□ _____

□ _____

Customer Contacts:

□ _____

□ _____

Builder Contacts:

□ _____

□ _____

Gratitude:

□ _____

JANUARY 10TH

□ Supplements   □ Water   □ Meditate/Mindset   □ Movement

To Do List:

□ _____

□ _____

□ _____

□ _____

□ _____

New Prospect Contacts:

□ _____

□ _____

Follow-Up Contacts:

□ _____

□ _____

Customer Contacts:

□ _____

□ _____

Builder Contacts:

□ _____

□ _____

Gratitude:

□ _____

JANUARY 11TH

□ Supplements   □ Water   □ Meditate/Mindset   □ Movement

To Do List:

□ _____

□ _____

□ _____

□ _____

□ _____

New Prospect Contacts:

□ _____

□ _____

Follow-Up Contacts:

□ _____

□ _____

Customer Contacts:

□ _____

□ _____

Builder Contacts:

□ _____

□ _____

Gratitude:

□ _____

JANUARY 12TH

☐ Supplements   ☐ Water   ☐ Meditate/Mindset   ☐ Movement

To Do List:

☐ _____

☐ _____

☐ _____

☐ _____

☐ _____

New Prospect Contacts:

☐ _____

☐ _____

Follow-Up Contacts:

☐ _____

☐ _____

Customer Contacts:

☐ _____

☐ _____

Builder Contacts:

☐ _____

☐ _____

Gratitude:

☐ _____

JANUARY 13TH

☐ Supplements   ☐ Water   ☐ Meditate/Mindset   ☐ Movement

To Do List:

☐ _____

☐ _____

☐ _____

☐ _____

☐ _____

New Prospect Contacts:

☐ _____

☐ _____

Follow-Up Contacts:

☐ _____

☐ _____

Customer Contacts:

☐ _____

☐ _____

Builder Contacts:

☐ _____

☐ _____

Gratitude:

☐ _____

JANUARY 14TH

□ Supplements   □ Water   □ Meditate/Mindset   □ Movement

To Do List:

□ _____

□ _____

□ _____

□ _____

□ _____

New Prospect Contacts:

□ _____

□ _____

Follow-Up Contacts:

□ _____

□ _____

Customer Contacts:

□ _____

□ _____

Builder Contacts:

□ _____

□ _____

Gratitude:

□ _____

JANUARY 15TH

☐ Supplements   ☐ Water   ☐ Meditate/Mindset   ☐ Movement

To Do List:

☐ _____

☐ _____

☐ _____

☐ _____

☐ _____

New Prospect Contacts:

☐ _____

☐ _____

Follow-Up Contacts:

☐ _____

☐ _____

Customer Contacts:

☐ _____

☐ _____

Builder Contacts:

☐ _____

☐ _____

Gratitude:

☐ _____

JANUARY 16TH

☐ Supplements   ☐ Water   ☐ Meditate/Mindset   ☐ Movement

To Do List:

☐ _____

☐ _____

☐ _____

☐ _____

☐ _____

New Prospect Contacts:

☐ _____

☐ _____

Follow-Up Contacts:

☐ _____

☐ _____

Customer Contacts:

☐ _____

☐ _____

Builder Contacts:

☐ _____

☐ _____

Gratitude:

☐ _____

JANUARY 17ᵀᴴ

☐ Supplements   ☐ Water   ☐ Meditate/Mindset   ☐ Movement

To Do List:

☐ _____

☐ _____

☐ _____

☐ _____

☐ _____

New Prospect Contacts:

☐ _____

☐ _____

Follow-Up Contacts:

☐ _____

☐ _____

Customer Contacts:

☐ _____

☐ _____

Builder Contacts:

☐ _____

☐ _____

Gratitude:

☐ _____

JANUARY 18TH

☐ Supplements   ☐ Water   ☐ Meditate/Mindset   ☐ Movement

To Do List:

☐ _____

☐ _____

☐ _____

☐ _____

☐ _____

New Prospect Contacts:

☐ _____

☐ _____

Follow-Up Contacts:

☐ _____

☐ _____

Customer Contacts:

☐ _____

☐ _____

Builder Contacts:

☐ _____

☐ _____

Gratitude:

☐ _____

JANUARY 19TH

□ Supplements   □ Water   □ Meditate/Mindset   □ Movement

To Do List:

□ _____

□ _____

□ _____

□ _____

□ _____

New Prospect Contacts:

□ _____

□ _____

Follow-Up Contacts:

□ _____

□ _____

Customer Contacts:

□ _____

□ _____

Builder Contacts:

□ _____

□ _____

Gratitude:

□ _____

JANUARY 20TH

□ Supplements   □ Water   □ Meditate/Mindset   □ Movement

To Do List:

□ _____

□ _____

□ _____

□ _____

□ _____

New Prospect Contacts:

□ _____

□ _____

Follow-Up Contacts:

□ _____

□ _____

Customer Contacts:

□ _____

□ _____

Builder Contacts:

□ _____

□ _____

Gratitude:

□ _____

JANUARY 21ST

□ Supplements   □ Water   □ Meditate/Mindset   □ Movement

To Do List:

□ _____
□ _____
□ _____
□ _____
□ _____

New Prospect Contacts:

□ _____
□ _____

Follow-Up Contacts:

□ _____
□ _____

Customer Contacts:

□ _____
□ _____

Builder Contacts:

□ _____
□ _____

Gratitude:

□ _____

JANUARY 22ND

☐ Supplements   ☐ Water   ☐ Meditate/Mindset   ☐ Movement

To Do List:

☐ _____

☐ _____

☐ _____

☐ _____

☐ _____

New Prospect Contacts:

☐ _____

☐ _____

Follow-Up Contacts:

☐ _____

☐ _____

Customer Contacts:

☐ _____

☐ _____

Builder Contacts:

☐ _____

☐ _____

Gratitude:

☐ _____

JANUARY 23RD

□ Supplements   □ Water   □ Meditate/Mindset   □ Movement

To Do List:

□ _____

□ _____

□ _____

□ _____

□ _____

New Prospect Contacts:

□ _____

□ _____

Follow-Up Contacts:

□ _____

□ _____

Customer Contacts:

□ _____

□ _____

Builder Contacts:

□ _____

□ _____

Gratitude:

□ _____

JANUARY 24TH

□ Supplements   □ Water   □ Meditate/Mindset   □ Movement

To Do List:

□ _____

□ _____

□ _____

□ _____

□ _____

New Prospect Contacts:

□ _____

□ _____

Follow-Up Contacts:

□ _____

□ _____

Customer Contacts:

□ _____

□ _____

Builder Contacts:

□ _____

□ _____

Gratitude:

□ _____

JANUARY 25TH

□ Supplements   □ Water   □ Meditate/Mindset   □ Movement

To Do List:

□ _____

□ _____

□ _____

□ _____

□ _____

New Prospect Contacts:

□ _____

□ _____

Follow-Up Contacts:

□ _____

□ _____

Customer Contacts:

□ _____

□ _____

Builder Contacts:

□ _____

□ _____

Gratitude:

□ _____

JANUARY 26TH

☐ Supplements   ☐ Water   ☐ Meditate/Mindset   ☐ Movement

To Do List:

☐ _____

☐ _____

☐ _____

☐ _____

☐ _____

New Prospect Contacts:

☐ _____

☐ _____

Follow-Up Contacts:

☐ _____

☐ _____

Customer Contacts:

☐ _____

☐ _____

Builder Contacts:

☐ _____

☐ _____

Gratitude:

☐ _____

JANUARY 27TH

□ Supplements   □ Water   □ Meditate/Mindset   □ Movement

To Do List:

□ _____

□ _____

□ _____

□ _____

□ _____

New Prospect Contacts:

□ _____

□ _____

Follow-Up Contacts:

□ _____

□ _____

Customer Contacts:

□ _____

□ _____

Builder Contacts:

□ _____

□ _____

Gratitude:

□ _____

JANUARY 28TH

☐ Supplements   ☐ Water   ☐ Meditate/Mindset   ☐ Movement

To Do List:

☐ _____

☐ _____

☐ _____

☐ _____

☐ _____

New Prospect Contacts:

☐ _____

☐ _____

Follow-Up Contacts:

☐ _____

☐ _____

Customer Contacts:

☐ _____

☐ _____

Builder Contacts:

☐ _____

☐ _____

Gratitude:

☐ _____

JANUARY 29TH

□ Supplements   □ Water   □ Meditate/Mindset   □ Movement

To Do List:

□ _____

□ _____

□ _____

□ _____

□ _____

New Prospect Contacts:

□ _____

□ _____

Follow-Up Contacts:

□ _____

□ _____

Customer Contacts:

□ _____

□ _____

Builder Contacts:

□ _____

□ _____

Gratitude:

□ _____

JANUARY 30TH

☐ Supplements   ☐ Water   ☐ Meditate/Mindset   ☐ Movement

To Do List:

☐ _____

☐ _____

☐ _____

☐ _____

☐ _____

New Prospect Contacts:

☐ _____

☐ _____

Follow-Up Contacts:

☐ _____

☐ _____

Customer Contacts:

☐ _____

☐ _____

Builder Contacts:

☐ _____

☐ _____

Gratitude:

☐ _____

JANUARY 31ST

To Do List:

- ☐ _____
- ☐ _____
- ☐ _____
- ☐ _____
- ☐ _____

New Prospect Contacts:

- ☐ _____
- ☐ _____

Follow-Up Contacts:

- ☐ _____
- ☐ _____

Customer Contacts:

- ☐ _____
- ☐ _____

Builder Contacts:

- ☐ _____
- ☐ _____

Gratitude:

- ☐ _____

FEBRUARY

FEBRUARY 1ˢᵀ

□ Supplements   □ Water   □ Meditate/Mindset   □ Movement

To Do List:

□ _____

□ _____

□ _____

□ _____

□ _____

New Prospect Contacts:

□ _____

□ _____

Follow-Up Contacts:

□ _____

□ _____

Customer Contacts:

□ _____

□ _____

Builder Contacts:

□ _____

□ _____

Gratitude:

□ _____

FEBRUARY 2ND

☐ Supplements   ☐ Water   ☐ Meditate/Mindset   ☐ Movement

To Do List:

☐ _____

☐ _____

☐ _____

☐ _____

☐ _____

New Prospect Contacts:

☐ _____

☐ _____

Follow-Up Contacts:

☐ _____

☐ _____

Customer Contacts:

☐ _____

☐ _____

Builder Contacts:

☐ _____

☐ _____

Gratitude:

☐ _____

FEBRUARY 3RD

□ Supplements   □ Water   □ Meditate/Mindset   □ Movement

To Do List:

□ _____
□ _____
□ _____
□ _____
□ _____

New Prospect Contacts:

□ _____
□ _____

Follow-Up Contacts:

□ _____
□ _____

Customer Contacts:

□ _____
□ _____

Builder Contacts:

□ _____
□ _____

Gratitude:

□ _____

FEBRUARY 4TH

☐ Supplements   ☐ Water   ☐ Meditate/Mindset   ☐ Movement

To Do List:

☐ _____

☐ _____

☐ _____

☐ _____

☐ _____

New Prospect Contacts:

☐ _____

☐ _____

Follow-Up Contacts:

☐ _____

☐ _____

Customer Contacts:

☐ _____

☐ _____

Builder Contacts:

☐ _____

☐ _____

Gratitude:

☐ _____

FEBRUARY 5TH

☐ Supplements   ☐ Water   ☐ Meditate/Mindset   ☐ Movement

To Do List:

☐ _____

☐ _____

☐ _____

☐ _____

☐ _____

New Prospect Contacts:

☐ _____

☐ _____

Follow-Up Contacts:

☐ _____

☐ _____

Customer Contacts:

☐ _____

☐ _____

Builder Contacts:

☐ _____

☐ _____

Gratitude:

☐ _____

FEBRUARY 6TH

☐ Supplements   ☐ Water   ☐ Meditate/Mindset   ☐ Movement

To Do List:

☐ _____
☐ _____
☐ _____
☐ _____
☐ _____

New Prospect Contacts:

☐ _____
☐ _____

Follow-Up Contacts:

☐ _____
☐ _____

Customer Contacts:

☐ _____
☐ _____

Builder Contacts:

☐ _____
☐ _____

Gratitude:

☐ _____

FEBRUARY 7TH

☐ Supplements ☐ Water ☐ Meditate/Mindset ☐ Movement

To Do List:

☐ _____

☐ _____

☐ _____

☐ _____

☐ _____

New Prospect Contacts:

☐ _____

☐ _____

Follow-Up Contacts:

☐ _____

☐ _____

Customer Contacts:

☐ _____

☐ _____

Builder Contacts:

☐ _____

☐ _____

Gratitude:

☐ _____

FEBRUARY 8TH

☐ Supplements ☐ Water ☐ Meditate/Mindset ☐ Movement

To Do List:

☐ _____

☐ _____

☐ _____

☐ _____

☐ _____

New Prospect Contacts:

☐ _____

☐ _____

Follow-Up Contacts:

☐ _____

☐ _____

Customer Contacts:

☐ _____

☐ _____

Builder Contacts:

☐ _____

☐ _____

Gratitude:

☐ _____

FEBRUARY 9TH

☐ Supplements   ☐ Water   ☐ Meditate/Mindset   ☐ Movement

To Do List:

☐ _____
☐ _____
☐ _____
☐ _____
☐ _____

New Prospect Contacts:

☐ _____
☐ _____

Follow-Up Contacts:

☐ _____
☐ _____

Customer Contacts:

☐ _____
☐ _____

Builder Contacts:

☐ _____
☐ _____

Gratitude:

☐ _____

FEBRUARY 10TH

☐ Supplements   ☐ Water   ☐ Meditate/Mindset   ☐ Movement

To Do List:

☐ _____

☐ _____

☐ _____

☐ _____

☐ _____

New Prospect Contacts:

☐ _____

☐ _____

Follow-Up Contacts:

☐ _____

☐ _____

Customer Contacts:

☐ _____

☐ _____

Builder Contacts:

☐ _____

☐ _____

Gratitude:

☐ _____

FEBRUARY 11TH

☐ Supplements   ☐ Water   ☐ Meditate/Mindset   ☐ Movement

To Do List:

☐ _____

☐ _____

☐ _____

☐ _____

☐ _____

New Prospect Contacts:

☐ _____

☐ _____

Follow-Up Contacts:

☐ _____

☐ _____

Customer Contacts:

☐ _____

☐ _____

Builder Contacts:

☐ _____

☐ _____

Gratitude:

☐ _____

FEBRUARY 12TH

☐ Supplements   ☐ Water   ☐ Meditate/Mindset   ☐ Movement

To Do List:

☐ _____

☐ _____

☐ _____

☐ _____

☐ _____

New Prospect Contacts:

☐ _____

☐ _____

Follow-Up Contacts:

☐ _____

☐ _____

Customer Contacts:

☐ _____

☐ _____

Builder Contacts:

☐ _____

☐ _____

Gratitude:

☐ _____

FEBRUARY 13TH

□ Supplements   □ Water   □ Meditate/Mindset   □ Movement

To Do List:

□ _____

□ _____

□ _____

□ _____

□ _____

New Prospect Contacts:

□ _____

□ _____

Follow-Up Contacts:

□ _____

□ _____

Customer Contacts:

□ _____

□ _____

Builder Contacts:

□ _____

□ _____

Gratitude:

□ _____

FEBRUARY 14TH

☐ Supplements ☐ Water ☐ Meditate/Mindset ☐ Movement

To Do List:

☐ _____

☐ _____

☐ _____

☐ _____

☐ _____

New Prospect Contacts:

☐ _____

☐ _____

Follow-Up Contacts:

☐ _____

☐ _____

Customer Contacts:

☐ _____

☐ _____

Builder Contacts:

☐ _____

☐ _____

Gratitude:

☐ _____

FEBRUARY 15TH

☐ Supplements   ☐ Water   ☐ Meditate/Mindset   ☐ Movement

To Do List:

☐ _____

☐ _____

☐ _____

☐ _____

☐ _____

New Prospect Contacts:

☐ _____

☐ _____

Follow-Up Contacts:

☐ _____

☐ _____

Customer Contacts:

☐ _____

☐ _____

Builder Contacts:

☐ _____

☐ _____

Gratitude:

☐ _____

FEBRUARY 16TH

☐ Supplements   ☐ Water   ☐ Meditate/Mindset   ☐ Movement

To Do List:

☐ _____

☐ _____

☐ _____

☐ _____

☐ _____

New Prospect Contacts:

☐ _____

☐ _____

Follow-Up Contacts:

☐ _____

☐ _____

Customer Contacts:

☐ _____

☐ _____

Builder Contacts:

☐ _____

☐ _____

Gratitude:

☐ _____

FEBRUARY 17TH

□ Supplements   □ Water   □ Meditate/Mindset   □ Movement

To Do List:

□ _____

□ _____

□ _____

□ _____

□ _____

New Prospect Contacts:

□ _____

□ _____

Follow-Up Contacts:

□ _____

□ _____

Customer Contacts:

□ _____

□ _____

Builder Contacts:

□ _____

□ _____

Gratitude:

□ _____

FEBRUARY 18TH

☐ Supplements ☐ Water ☐ Meditate/Mindset ☐ Movement

To Do List:

☐ _____

☐ _____

☐ _____

☐ _____

☐ _____

New Prospect Contacts:

☐ _____

☐ _____

Follow-Up Contacts:

☐ _____

☐ _____

Customer Contacts:

☐ _____

☐ _____

Builder Contacts:

☐ _____

☐ _____

Gratitude:

☐ _____

FEBRUARY 19TH

☐ Supplements   ☐ Water   ☐ Meditate/Mindset   ☐ Movement

To Do List:

☐ _____

☐ _____

☐ _____

☐ _____

☐ _____

New Prospect Contacts:

☐ _____

☐ _____

Follow-Up Contacts:

☐ _____

☐ _____

Customer Contacts:

☐ _____

☐ _____

Builder Contacts:

☐ _____

☐ _____

Gratitude:

☐ _____

FEBRUARY 20TH

☐ Supplements   ☐ Water   ☐ Meditate/Mindset   ☐ Movement

To Do List:

☐ _____

☐ _____

☐ _____

☐ _____

☐ _____

New Prospect Contacts:

☐ _____

☐ _____

Follow-Up Contacts:

☐ _____

☐ _____

Customer Contacts:

☐ _____

☐ _____

Builder Contacts:

☐ _____

☐ _____

Gratitude:

☐ _____

FEBRUARY 21ST

☐ Supplements   ☐ Water   ☐ Meditate/Mindset   ☐ Movement

To Do List:

☐ _____

☐ _____

☐ _____

☐ _____

☐ _____

New Prospect Contacts:

☐ _____

☐ _____

Follow-Up Contacts:

☐ _____

☐ _____

Customer Contacts:

☐ _____

☐ _____

Builder Contacts:

☐ _____

☐ _____

Gratitude:

☐ _____

FEBRUARY 22ND

□ Supplements   □ Water   □ Meditate/Mindset   □ Movement

To Do List:

□ _____

□ _____

□ _____

□ _____

□ _____

New Prospect Contacts:

□ _____

□ _____

Follow-Up Contacts:

□ _____

□ _____

Customer Contacts:

□ _____

□ _____

Builder Contacts:

□ _____

□ _____

Gratitude:

□ _____

FEBRUARY 23RD

☐ Supplements   ☐ Water   ☐ Meditate/Mindset   ☐ Movement

To Do List:

☐ _____
☐ _____
☐ _____
☐ _____
☐ _____

New Prospect Contacts:

☐ _____
☐ _____

Follow-Up Contacts:

☐ _____
☐ _____

Customer Contacts:

☐ _____
☐ _____

Builder Contacts:

☐ _____
☐ _____

Gratitude:

☐ _____

FEBRUARY 24TH

☐ Supplements ☐ Water ☐ Meditate/Mindset ☐ Movement

To Do List:

☐ _____

☐ _____

☐ _____

☐ _____

☐ _____

New Prospect Contacts:

☐ _____

☐ _____

Follow-Up Contacts:

☐ _____

☐ _____

Customer Contacts:

☐ _____

☐ _____

Builder Contacts:

☐ _____

☐ _____

Gratitude:

☐ _____

FEBRUARY 25TH

☐ Supplements   ☐ Water   ☐ Meditate/Mindset   ☐ Movement

To Do List:

☐ _____
☐ _____
☐ _____
☐ _____
☐ _____

New Prospect Contacts:

☐ _____
☐ _____

Follow-Up Contacts:

☐ _____
☐ _____

Customer Contacts:

☐ _____
☐ _____

Builder Contacts:

☐ _____
☐ _____

Gratitude:

☐ _____

FEBRUARY 26TH

☐ Supplements   ☐ Water   ☐ Meditate/Mindset   ☐ Movement

To Do List:

☐ _____

☐ _____

☐ _____

☐ _____

☐ _____

New Prospect Contacts:

☐ _____

☐ _____

Follow-Up Contacts:

☐ _____

☐ _____

Customer Contacts:

☐ _____

☐ _____

Builder Contacts:

☐ _____

☐ _____

Gratitude:

☐ _____

FEBRUARY 27TH

□ Supplements   □ Water   □ Meditate/Mindset   □ Movement

To Do List:

□ _____
□ _____
□ _____
□ _____
□ _____

New Prospect Contacts:

□ _____
□ _____

Follow-Up Contacts:

□ _____
□ _____

Customer Contacts:

□ _____
□ _____

Builder Contacts:

□ _____
□ _____

Gratitude:

□ _____

FEBRUARY 28TH

☐ Supplements   ☐ Water   ☐ Meditate/Mindset   ☐ Movement

To Do List:

☐ _____

☐ _____

☐ _____

☐ _____

☐ _____

New Prospect Contacts:

☐ _____

☐ _____

Follow-Up Contacts:

☐ _____

☐ _____

Customer Contacts:

☐ _____

☐ _____

Builder Contacts:

☐ _____

☐ _____

Gratitude:

☐ _____

MARCH

MARCH 1ST

To Do List:

☐ _____

☐ _____

☐ _____

☐ _____

☐ _____

New Prospect Contacts:

☐ _____

☐ _____

Follow-Up Contacts:

☐ _____

☐ _____

Customer Contacts:

☐ _____

☐ _____

Builder Contacts:

☐ _____

☐ _____

Gratitude:

☐ _____

March 2nd

To Do List:

☐ _____

☐ _____

☐ _____

☐ _____

☐ _____

New Prospect Contacts:

☐ _____

☐ _____

Follow-Up Contacts:

☐ _____

☐ _____

Customer Contacts:

☐ _____

☐ _____

Builder Contacts:

☐ _____

☐ _____

Gratitude:

☐ _____

MARCH 3RD

□ Supplements   □ Water   □ Meditate/Mindset   □ Movement

To Do List:

□ _____

□ _____

□ _____

□ _____

□ _____

New Prospect Contacts:

□ _____

□ _____

Follow-Up Contacts:

□ _____

□ _____

Customer Contacts:

□ _____

□ _____

Builder Contacts:

□ _____

□ _____

Gratitude:

□ _____

MARCH 4TH

To Do List:

☐ _____
☐ _____
☐ _____
☐ _____
☐ _____

New Prospect Contacts:

☐ _____
☐ _____

Follow-Up Contacts:

☐ _____
☐ _____

Customer Contacts:

☐ _____
☐ _____

Builder Contacts:

☐ _____
☐ _____

Gratitude:

☐ _____

MARCH 5TH

☐ Supplements   ☐ Water   ☐ Meditate/Mindset   ☐ Movement

To Do List:

☐ _____

☐ _____

☐ _____

☐ _____

☐ _____

New Prospect Contacts:

☐ _____

☐ _____

Follow-Up Contacts:

☐ _____

☐ _____

Customer Contacts:

☐ _____

☐ _____

Builder Contacts:

☐ _____

☐ _____

Gratitude:

☐ _____

MARCH 6TH

□ Supplements   □ Water   □ Meditate/Mindset   □ Movement

To Do List:

□ _____

□ _____

□ _____

□ _____

□ _____

New Prospect Contacts:

□ _____

□ _____

Follow-Up Contacts:

□ _____

□ _____

Customer Contacts:

□ _____

□ _____

Builder Contacts:

□ _____

□ _____

Gratitude:

□ _____

MARCH 7TH

☐ Supplements   ☐ Water   ☐ Meditate/Mindset   ☐ Movement

To Do List:

☐ _____

☐ _____

☐ _____

☐ _____

☐ _____

New Prospect Contacts:

☐ _____

☐ _____

Follow-Up Contacts:

☐ _____

☐ _____

Customer Contacts:

☐ _____

☐ _____

Builder Contacts:

☐ _____

☐ _____

Gratitude:

☐ _____

MARCH 8TH

□ Supplements   □ Water   □ Meditate/Mindset   □ Movement

To Do List:

□ _____

□ _____

□ _____

□ _____

□ _____

New Prospect Contacts:

□ _____

□ _____

Follow-Up Contacts:

□ _____

□ _____

Customer Contacts:

□ _____

□ _____

Builder Contacts:

□ _____

□ _____

Gratitude:

□ _____

MARCH 9TH

☐ Supplements   ☐ Water   ☐ Meditate/Mindset   ☐ Movement

To Do List:

☐ _____

☐ _____

☐ _____

☐ _____

☐ _____

New Prospect Contacts:

☐ _____

☐ _____

Follow-Up Contacts:

☐ _____

☐ _____

Customer Contacts:

☐ _____

☐ _____

Builder Contacts:

☐ _____

☐ _____

Gratitude:

☐ _____

MARCH 10TH

□ Supplements   □ Water   □ Meditate/Mindset   □ Movement

To Do List:

□ _____

□ _____

□ _____

□ _____

□ _____

New Prospect Contacts:

□ _____

□ _____

Follow-Up Contacts:

□ _____

□ _____

Customer Contacts:

□ _____

□ _____

Builder Contacts:

□ _____

□ _____

Gratitude:

□ _____

MARCH 11TH

□ Supplements   □ Water   □ Meditate/Mindset   □ Movement

To Do List:

□ _____

□ _____

□ _____

□ _____

□ _____

New Prospect Contacts:

□ _____

□ _____

Follow-Up Contacts:

□ _____

□ _____

Customer Contacts:

□ _____

□ _____

Builder Contacts:

□ _____

□ _____

Gratitude:

□ _____

MARCH 12TH

□ Supplements   □ Water   □ Meditate/Mindset   □ Movement

To Do List:

□ _____

□ _____

□ _____

□ _____

□ _____

New Prospect Contacts:

□ _____

□ _____

Follow-Up Contacts:

□ _____

□ _____

Customer Contacts:

□ _____

□ _____

Builder Contacts:

□ _____

□ _____

Gratitude:

□ _____

MARCH 13TH

□ Supplements   □ Water   □ Meditate/Mindset   □ Movement

To Do List:

□ _____

□ _____

□ _____

□ _____

□ _____

New Prospect Contacts:

□ _____

□ _____

Follow-Up Contacts:

□ _____

□ _____

Customer Contacts:

□ _____

□ _____

Builder Contacts:

□ _____

□ _____

Gratitude:

□ _____

MARCH 14TH

□ Supplements   □ Water   □ Meditate/Mindset   □ Movement

To Do List:

□ _____

□ _____

□ _____

□ _____

□ _____

New Prospect Contacts:

□ _____

□ _____

Follow-Up Contacts:

□ _____

□ _____

Customer Contacts:

□ _____

□ _____

Builder Contacts:

□ _____

□ _____

Gratitude:

□ _____

MARCH 15ᵀᴴ

□ Supplements   □ Water   □ Meditate/Mindset   □ Movement

To Do List:

□ _____

□ _____

□ _____

□ _____

□ _____

New Prospect Contacts:

□ _____

□ _____

Follow-Up Contacts:

□ _____

□ _____

Customer Contacts:

□ _____

□ _____

Builder Contacts:

□ _____

□ _____

Gratitude:

□ _____

MARCH 16TH

☐ Supplements   ☐ Water   ☐ Meditate/Mindset   ☐ Movement

To Do List:

☐ _____

☐ _____

☐ _____

☐ _____

☐ _____

New Prospect Contacts:

☐ _____

☐ _____

Follow-Up Contacts:

☐ _____

☐ _____

Customer Contacts:

☐ _____

☐ _____

Builder Contacts:

☐ _____

☐ _____

Gratitude:

☐ _____

MARCH 17TH

☐ Supplements   ☐ Water   ☐ Meditate/Mindset   ☐ Movement

To Do List:

☐ _____

☐ _____

☐ _____

☐ _____

☐ _____

New Prospect Contacts:

☐ _____

☐ _____

Follow-Up Contacts:

☐ _____

☐ _____

Customer Contacts:

☐ _____

☐ _____

Builder Contacts:

☐ _____

☐ _____

Gratitude:

☐ _____

MARCH 18TH

☐ Supplements   ☐ Water   ☐ Meditate/Mindset   ☐ Movement

To Do List:

☐ _____

☐ _____

☐ _____

☐ _____

☐ _____

New Prospect Contacts:

☐ _____

☐ _____

Follow-Up Contacts:

☐ _____

☐ _____

Customer Contacts:

☐ _____

☐ _____

Builder Contacts:

☐ _____

☐ _____

Gratitude:

☐ _____

MARCH 19TH

□ Supplements   □ Water   □ Meditate/Mindset   □ Movement

To Do List:

□ _____

□ _____

□ _____

□ _____

□ _____

New Prospect Contacts:

□ _____

□ _____

Follow-Up Contacts:

□ _____

□ _____

Customer Contacts:

□ _____

□ _____

Builder Contacts:

□ _____

□ _____

Gratitude:

□ _____

MARCH 20TH

☐ Supplements   ☐ Water   ☐ Meditate/Mindset   ☐ Movement

To Do List:

☐ _____

☐ _____

☐ _____

☐ _____

☐ _____

New Prospect Contacts:

☐ _____

☐ _____

Follow-Up Contacts:

☐ _____

☐ _____

Customer Contacts:

☐ _____

☐ _____

Builder Contacts:

☐ _____

☐ _____

Gratitude:

☐ _____

MARCH 21ST

□ Supplements   □ Water   □ Meditate/Mindset   □ Movement

To Do List:

□ _____

□ _____

□ _____

□ _____

□ _____

New Prospect Contacts:

□ _____

□ _____

Follow-Up Contacts:

□ _____

□ _____

Customer Contacts:

□ _____

□ _____

Builder Contacts:

□ _____

□ _____

Gratitude:

□ _____

MARCH 22ND

To Do List:

□ _____

□ _____

□ _____

□ _____

□ _____

New Prospect Contacts:

□ _____

□ _____

Follow-Up Contacts:

□ _____

□ _____

Customer Contacts:

□ _____

□ _____

Builder Contacts:

□ _____

□ _____

Gratitude:

□ _____

MARCH 23RD

☐ Supplements   ☐ Water   ☐ Meditate/Mindset   ☐ Movement

To Do List:

☐ _____

☐ _____

☐ _____

☐ _____

☐ _____

New Prospect Contacts:

☐ _____

☐ _____

Follow-Up Contacts:

☐ _____

☐ _____

Customer Contacts:

☐ _____

☐ _____

Builder Contacts:

☐ _____

☐ _____

Gratitude:

☐ _____

MARCH 24TH

□ Supplements   □ Water   □ Meditate/Mindset   □ Movement

To Do List:

□ _____
□ _____
□ _____
□ _____
□ _____

New Prospect Contacts:

□ _____
□ _____

Follow-Up Contacts:

□ _____
□ _____

Customer Contacts:

□ _____
□ _____

Builder Contacts:

□ _____
□ _____

Gratitude:

□ _____

MARCH 25TH

□ Supplements   □ Water   □ Meditate/Mindset   □ Movement

To Do List:

- □ _____
- □ _____
- □ _____
- □ _____
- □ _____

New Prospect Contacts:

- □ _____
- □ _____

Follow-Up Contacts:

- □ _____
- □ _____

Customer Contacts:

- □ _____
- □ _____

Builder Contacts:

- □ _____
- □ _____

Gratitude:

- □ _____

MARCH 26TH

☐ Supplements   ☐ Water   ☐ Meditate/Mindset   ☐ Movement

To Do List:

☐ _____

☐ _____

☐ _____

☐ _____

☐ _____

New Prospect Contacts:

☐ _____

☐ _____

Follow-Up Contacts:

☐ _____

☐ _____

Customer Contacts:

☐ _____

☐ _____

Builder Contacts:

☐ _____

☐ _____

Gratitude:

☐ _____

MARCH 27TH

☐ Supplements   ☐ Water   ☐ Meditate/Mindset   ☐ Movement

To Do List:

☐ _____

☐ _____

☐ _____

☐ _____

☐ _____

New Prospect Contacts:

☐ _____

☐ _____

Follow-Up Contacts:

☐ _____

☐ _____

Customer Contacts:

☐ _____

☐ _____

Builder Contacts:

☐ _____

☐ _____

Gratitude:

☐ _____

MARCH 28TH

□ Supplements   □ Water   □ Meditate/Mindset   □ Movement

To Do List:

□ _____

□ _____

□ _____

□ _____

□ _____

New Prospect Contacts:

□ _____

□ _____

Follow-Up Contacts:

□ _____

□ _____

Customer Contacts:

□ _____

□ _____

Builder Contacts:

□ _____

□ _____

Gratitude:

□ _____

MARCH 29TH

□ Supplements   □ Water   □ Meditate/Mindset   □ Movement

To Do List:

□ _____

□ _____

□ _____

□ _____

□ _____

New Prospect Contacts:

□ _____

□ _____

Follow-Up Contacts:

□ _____

□ _____

Customer Contacts:

□ _____

□ _____

Builder Contacts:

□ _____

□ _____

Gratitude:

□ _____

MARCH 30TH

☐ Supplements   ☐ Water   ☐ Meditate/Mindset   ☐ Movement

To Do List:

☐ _____

☐ _____

☐ _____

☐ _____

☐ _____

New Prospect Contacts:

☐ _____

☐ _____

Follow-Up Contacts:

☐ _____

☐ _____

Customer Contacts:

☐ _____

☐ _____

Builder Contacts:

☐ _____

☐ _____

Gratitude:

☐ _____

MARCH 31ST

To Do List:

□ _____

□ _____

□ _____

□ _____

□ _____

New Prospect Contacts:

□ _____

□ _____

Follow-Up Contacts:

□ _____

□ _____

Customer Contacts:

□ _____

□ _____

Builder Contacts:

□ _____

□ _____

Gratitude:

□ _____

APRIL

APRIL 1ST

☐ Supplements   ☐ Water   ☐ Meditate/Mindset   ☐ Movement

To Do List:

☐ _____
☐ _____
☐ _____
☐ _____
☐ _____

New Prospect Contacts:

☐ _____
☐ _____

Follow-Up Contacts:

☐ _____
☐ _____

Customer Contacts:

☐ _____
☐ _____

Builder Contacts:

☐ _____
☐ _____

Gratitude:

☐ _____

APRIL 2ND

☐ Supplements   ☐ Water   ☐ Meditate/Mindset   ☐ Movement

To Do List:

☐ _____

☐ _____

☐ _____

☐ _____

☐ _____

New Prospect Contacts:

☐ _____

☐ _____

Follow-Up Contacts:

☐ _____

☐ _____

Customer Contacts:

☐ _____

☐ _____

Builder Contacts:

☐ _____

☐ _____

Gratitude:

☐ _____

APRIL 3RD

☐ Supplements ☐ Water ☐ Meditate/Mindset ☐ Movement

To Do List:

☐ _____

☐ _____

☐ _____

☐ _____

☐ _____

New Prospect Contacts:

☐ _____

☐ _____

Follow-Up Contacts:

☐ _____

☐ _____

Customer Contacts:

☐ _____

☐ _____

Builder Contacts:

☐ _____

☐ _____

Gratitude:

☐ _____

APRIL 4TH

To Do List:

☐ _____

☐ _____

☐ _____

☐ _____

☐ _____

New Prospect Contacts:

☐ _____

☐ _____

Follow-Up Contacts:

☐ _____

☐ _____

Customer Contacts:

☐ _____

☐ _____

Builder Contacts:

☐ _____

☐ _____

Gratitude:

☐ _____

APRIL 5TH

☐ Supplements   ☐ Water   ☐ Meditate/Mindset   ☐ Movement

To Do List:

☐ _____

☐ _____

☐ _____

☐ _____

☐ _____

New Prospect Contacts:

☐ _____

☐ _____

Follow-Up Contacts:

☐ _____

☐ _____

Customer Contacts:

☐ _____

☐ _____

Builder Contacts:

☐ _____

☐ _____

Gratitude:

☐ _____

APRIL 6TH

□ Supplements   □ Water   □ Meditate/Mindset   □ Movement

To Do List:

□ _____

□ _____

□ _____

□ _____

□ _____

New Prospect Contacts:

□ _____

□ _____

Follow-Up Contacts:

□ _____

□ _____

Customer Contacts:

□ _____

□ _____

Builder Contacts:

□ _____

□ _____

Gratitude:

□ _____

APRIL 7TH

☐ Supplements   ☐ Water   ☐ Meditate/Mindset   ☐ Movement

To Do List:

☐ _____
☐ _____
☐ _____
☐ _____
☐ _____

New Prospect Contacts:

☐ _____
☐ _____

Follow-Up Contacts:

☐ _____
☐ _____

Customer Contacts:

☐ _____
☐ _____

Builder Contacts:

☐ _____
☐ _____

Gratitude:

☐ _____

APRIL 8TH

□ Supplements   □ Water   □ Meditate/Mindset   □ Movement

To Do List:

□ _____

□ _____

□ _____

□ _____

□ _____

New Prospect Contacts:

□ _____

□ _____

Follow-Up Contacts:

□ _____

□ _____

Customer Contacts:

□ _____

□ _____

Builder Contacts:

□ _____

□ _____

Gratitude:

□ _____

APRIL 9TH

☐ Supplements   ☐ Water   ☐ Meditate/Mindset   ☐ Movement

To Do List:

☐ _____

☐ _____

☐ _____

☐ _____

☐ _____

New Prospect Contacts:

☐ _____

☐ _____

Follow-Up Contacts:

☐ _____

☐ _____

Customer Contacts:

☐ _____

☐ _____

Builder Contacts:

☐ _____

☐ _____

Gratitude:

☐ _____

APRIL 10TH

□ Supplements   □ Water   □ Meditate/Mindset   □ Movement

To Do List:

□ _____

□ _____

□ _____

□ _____

□ _____

New Prospect Contacts:

□ _____

□ _____

Follow-Up Contacts:

□ _____

□ _____

Customer Contacts:

□ _____

□ _____

Builder Contacts:

□ _____

□ _____

Gratitude:

□ _____

APRIL 11TH

□ Supplements   □ Water   □ Meditate/Mindset   □ Movement

To Do List:

□ _____

□ _____

□ _____

□ _____

□ _____

New Prospect Contacts:

□ _____

□ _____

Follow-Up Contacts:

□ _____

□ _____

Customer Contacts:

□ _____

□ _____

Builder Contacts:

□ _____

□ _____

Gratitude:

□ _____

APRIL 12TH

☐ Supplements   ☐ Water   ☐ Meditate/Mindset   ☐ Movement

To Do List:

☐ _____

☐ _____

☐ _____

☐ _____

☐ _____

New Prospect Contacts:

☐ _____

☐ _____

Follow-Up Contacts:

☐ _____

☐ _____

Customer Contacts:

☐ _____

☐ _____

Builder Contacts:

☐ _____

☐ _____

Gratitude:

☐ _____

APRIL 13TH

☐ Supplements   ☐ Water   ☐ Meditate/Mindset   ☐ Movement

To Do List:

☐ _____

☐ _____

☐ _____

☐ _____

☐ _____

New Prospect Contacts:

☐ _____

☐ _____

Follow-Up Contacts:

☐ _____

☐ _____

Customer Contacts:

☐ _____

☐ _____

Builder Contacts:

☐ _____

☐ _____

Gratitude:

☐ _____

APRIL 14TH

☐ Supplements   ☐ Water   ☐ Meditate/Mindset   ☐ Movement

To Do List:

☐ _____

☐ _____

☐ _____

☐ _____

☐ _____

New Prospect Contacts:

☐ _____

☐ _____

Follow-Up Contacts:

☐ _____

☐ _____

Customer Contacts:

☐ _____

☐ _____

Builder Contacts:

☐ _____

☐ _____

Gratitude:

☐ _____

APRIL 15TH

☐ Supplements   ☐ Water   ☐ Meditate/Mindset   ☐ Movement

To Do List:

☐ _____

☐ _____

☐ _____

☐ _____

☐ _____

New Prospect Contacts:

☐ _____

☐ _____

Follow-Up Contacts:

☐ _____

☐ _____

Customer Contacts:

☐ _____

☐ _____

Builder Contacts:

☐ _____

☐ _____

Gratitude:

☐ _____

APRIL 16TH

□ Supplements   □ Water   □ Meditate/Mindset   □ Movement

To Do List:

□ _____

□ _____

□ _____

□ _____

□ _____

New Prospect Contacts:

□ _____

□ _____

Follow-Up Contacts:

□ _____

□ _____

Customer Contacts:

□ _____

□ _____

Builder Contacts:

□ _____

□ _____

Gratitude:

□ _____

APRIL 17TH

□ Supplements □ Water □ Meditate/Mindset □ Movement

To Do List:

□ _____
□ _____
□ _____
□ _____
□ _____

New Prospect Contacts:

□ _____
□ _____

Follow-Up Contacts:

□ _____
□ _____

Customer Contacts:

□ _____
□ _____

Builder Contacts:

□ _____
□ _____

Gratitude:

□ _____

APRIL 18TH

☐ Supplements   ☐ Water   ☐ Meditate/Mindset   ☐ Movement

To Do List:

☐ _____
☐ _____
☐ _____
☐ _____
☐ _____

New Prospect Contacts:

☐ _____
☐ _____

Follow-Up Contacts:

☐ _____
☐ _____

Customer Contacts:

☐ _____
☐ _____

Builder Contacts:

☐ _____
☐ _____

Gratitude:

☐ _____

APRIL 19TH

□ Supplements   □ Water   □ Meditate/Mindset   □ Movement

To Do List:

□ _____
□ _____
□ _____
□ _____
□ _____

New Prospect Contacts:

□ _____
□ _____

Follow-Up Contacts:

□ _____
□ _____

Customer Contacts:

□ _____
□ _____

Builder Contacts:

□ _____
□ _____

Gratitude:

□ _____

APRIL 20TH

☐ Supplements   ☐ Water   ☐ Meditate/Mindset   ☐ Movement

To Do List:

☐ _____

☐ _____

☐ _____

☐ _____

☐ _____

New Prospect Contacts:

☐ _____

☐ _____

Follow-Up Contacts:

☐ _____

☐ _____

Customer Contacts:

☐ _____

☐ _____

Builder Contacts:

☐ _____

☐ _____

Gratitude:

☐ _____

APRIL 21ST

☐ Supplements   ☐ Water   ☐ Meditate/Mindset   ☐ Movement

To Do List:

☐ _____

☐ _____

☐ _____

☐ _____

☐ _____

New Prospect Contacts:

☐ _____

☐ _____

Follow-Up Contacts:

☐ _____

☐ _____

Customer Contacts:

☐ _____

☐ _____

Builder Contacts:

☐ _____

☐ _____

Gratitude:

☐ _____

APRIL 22ND

☐ Supplements   ☐ Water   ☐ Meditate/Mindset   ☐ Movement

To Do List:

☐ _____

☐ _____

☐ _____

☐ _____

☐ _____

New Prospect Contacts:

☐ _____

☐ _____

Follow-Up Contacts:

☐ _____

☐ _____

Customer Contacts:

☐ _____

☐ _____

Builder Contacts:

☐ _____

☐ _____

Gratitude:

☐ _____

APRIL 23RD

☐ Supplements   ☐ Water   ☐ Meditate/Mindset   ☐ Movement

To Do List:

☐ _____

☐ _____

☐ _____

☐ _____

☐ _____

New Prospect Contacts:

☐ _____

☐ _____

Follow-Up Contacts:

☐ _____

☐ _____

Customer Contacts:

☐ _____

☐ _____

Builder Contacts:

☐ _____

☐ _____

Gratitude:

☐ _____

APRIL 24TH

□ Supplements   □ Water   □ Meditate/Mindset   □ Movement

To Do List:

□ _____

□ _____

□ _____

□ _____

□ _____

New Prospect Contacts:

□ _____

□ _____

Follow-Up Contacts:

□ _____

□ _____

Customer Contacts:

□ _____

□ _____

Builder Contacts:

□ _____

□ _____

Gratitude:

□ _____

APRIL 25TH

□ Supplements   □ Water   □ Meditate/Mindset   □ Movement

To Do List:

□ _____

□ _____

□ _____

□ _____

□ _____

New Prospect Contacts:

□ _____

□ _____

Follow-Up Contacts:

□ _____

□ _____

Customer Contacts:

□ _____

□ _____

Builder Contacts:

□ _____

□ _____

Gratitude:

□ _____

APRIL 26TH

☐ Supplements   ☐ Water   ☐ Meditate/Mindset   ☐ Movement

To Do List:

☐ _____
☐ _____
☐ _____
☐ _____
☐ _____

New Prospect Contacts:

☐ _____
☐ _____

Follow-Up Contacts:

☐ _____
☐ _____

Customer Contacts:

☐ _____
☐ _____

Builder Contacts:

☐ _____
☐ _____

Gratitude:

☐ _____

APRIL 27TH

□ Supplements   □ Water   □ Meditate/Mindset   □ Movement

To Do List:

□ _____
□ _____
□ _____
□ _____
□ _____

New Prospect Contacts:

□ _____
□ _____

Follow-Up Contacts:

□ _____
□ _____

Customer Contacts:

□ _____
□ _____

Builder Contacts:

□ _____
□ _____

Gratitude:

□ _____

APRIL 28TH

□ Supplements   □ Water   □ Meditate/Mindset   □ Movement

To Do List:

□ _____
□ _____
□ _____
□ _____
□ _____

New Prospect Contacts:

□ _____
□ _____

Follow-Up Contacts:

□ _____
□ _____

Customer Contacts:

□ _____
□ _____

Builder Contacts:

□ _____
□ _____

Gratitude:

□ _____

MAY

MAY 5TH

☐ Supplements   ☐ Water   ☐ Meditate/Mindset   ☐ Movement

To Do List:

☐ _____

☐ _____

☐ _____

☐ _____

☐ _____

New Prospect Contacts:

☐ _____

☐ _____

Follow-Up Contacts:

☐ _____

☐ _____

Customer Contacts:

☐ _____

☐ _____

Builder Contacts:

☐ _____

☐ _____

Gratitude:

☐ _____

MAY 6TH

☐ Supplements   ☐ Water   ☐ Meditate/Mindset   ☐ Movement

To Do List:

☐ _____
☐ _____
☐ _____
☐ _____
☐ _____

New Prospect Contacts:

☐ _____
☐ _____

Follow-Up Contacts:

☐ _____
☐ _____

Customer Contacts:

☐ _____
☐ _____

Builder Contacts:

☐ _____
☐ _____

Gratitude:

☐ _____

MAY 7TH

☐ Supplements   ☐ Water   ☐ Meditate/Mindset   ☐ Movement

To Do List:

☐ _____

☐ _____

☐ _____

☐ _____

☐ _____

New Prospect Contacts:

☐ _____

☐ _____

Follow-Up Contacts:

☐ _____

☐ _____

Customer Contacts:

☐ _____

☐ _____

Builder Contacts:

☐ _____

☐ _____

Gratitude:

☐ _____

MAY 8TH

□ Supplements   □ Water   □ Meditate/Mindset   □ Movement

To Do List:

□ _____
□ _____
□ _____
□ _____
□ _____

New Prospect Contacts:

□ _____
□ _____

Follow-Up Contacts:

□ _____
□ _____

Customer Contacts:

□ _____
□ _____

Builder Contacts:

□ _____
□ _____

Gratitude:

□ _____

MAY 9TH

☐ Supplements   ☐ Water   ☐ Meditate/Mindset   ☐ Movement

To Do List:

☐ _____

☐ _____

☐ _____

☐ _____

☐ _____

New Prospect Contacts:

☐ _____

☐ _____

Follow-Up Contacts:

☐ _____

☐ _____

Customer Contacts:

☐ _____

☐ _____

Builder Contacts:

☐ _____

☐ _____

Gratitude:

☐ _____

MAY 10TH

☐ Supplements ☐ Water ☐ Meditate/Mindset ☐ Movement

To Do List:

☐ _____

☐ _____

☐ _____

☐ _____

☐ _____

New Prospect Contacts:

☐ _____

☐ _____

Follow-Up Contacts:

☐ _____

☐ _____

Customer Contacts:

☐ _____

☐ _____

Builder Contacts:

☐ _____

☐ _____

Gratitude:

☐ _____

MAY 11TH

☐ Supplements ☐ Water ☐ Meditate/Mindset ☐ Movement

To Do List:

☐ _____

☐ _____

☐ _____

☐ _____

☐ _____

New Prospect Contacts:

☐ _____

☐ _____

Follow-Up Contacts:

☐ _____

☐ _____

Customer Contacts:

☐ _____

☐ _____

Builder Contacts:

☐ _____

☐ _____

Gratitude:

☐ _____

MAY 12TH

☐ Supplements   ☐ Water   ☐ Meditate/Mindset   ☐ Movement

To Do List:

☐ _____

☐ _____

☐ _____

☐ _____

☐ _____

New Prospect Contacts:

☐ _____

☐ _____

Follow-Up Contacts:

☐ _____

☐ _____

Customer Contacts:

☐ _____

☐ _____

Builder Contacts:

☐ _____

☐ _____

Gratitude:

☐ _____

MAY 13TH

□ Supplements   □ Water   □ Meditate/Mindset   □ Movement

To Do List:

□ _____

□ _____

□ _____

□ _____

□ _____

New Prospect Contacts:

□ _____

□ _____

Follow-Up Contacts:

□ _____

□ _____

Customer Contacts:

□ _____

□ _____

Builder Contacts:

□ _____

□ _____

Gratitude:

□ _____

MAY 14TH

☐ Supplements　　☐ Water　　☐ Meditate/Mindset　　☐ Movement

To Do List:

☐ _____

☐ _____

☐ _____

☐ _____

☐ _____

New Prospect Contacts:

☐ _____

☐ _____

Follow-Up Contacts:

☐ _____

☐ _____

Customer Contacts:

☐ _____

☐ _____

Builder Contacts:

☐ _____

☐ _____

Gratitude:

☐ _____

MAY 15TH

☐ Supplements   ☐ Water   ☐ Meditate/Mindset   ☐ Movement

To Do List:

☐ _____

☐ _____

☐ _____

☐ _____

☐ _____

New Prospect Contacts:

☐ _____

☐ _____

Follow-Up Contacts:

☐ _____

☐ _____

Customer Contacts:

☐ _____

☐ _____

Builder Contacts:

☐ _____

☐ _____

Gratitude:

☐ _____

MAY 16TH

□ Supplements   □ Water   □ Meditate/Mindset   □ Movement

To Do List:

□ _____

□ _____

□ _____

□ _____

□ _____

New Prospect Contacts:

□ _____

□ _____

Follow-Up Contacts:

□ _____

□ _____

Customer Contacts:

□ _____

□ _____

Builder Contacts:

□ _____

□ _____

Gratitude:

□ _____

MAY 17TH

□ Supplements   □ Water   □ Meditate/Mindset   □ Movement

To Do List:

□ _____

□ _____

□ _____

□ _____

□ _____

New Prospect Contacts:

□ _____

□ _____

Follow-Up Contacts:

□ _____

□ _____

Customer Contacts:

□ _____

□ _____

Builder Contacts:

□ _____

□ _____

Gratitude:

□ _____

MAY 18TH

☐ Supplements   ☐ Water   ☐ Meditate/Mindset   ☐ Movement

To Do List:

☐ _____

☐ _____

☐ _____

☐ _____

☐ _____

New Prospect Contacts:

☐ _____

☐ _____

Follow-Up Contacts:

☐ _____

☐ _____

Customer Contacts:

☐ _____

☐ _____

Builder Contacts:

☐ _____

☐ _____

Gratitude:

☐ _____

MAY 19TH

□ Supplements □ Water □ Meditate/Mindset □ Movement

To Do List:

□ _____
□ _____
□ _____
□ _____
□ _____

New Prospect Contacts:

□ _____
□ _____

Follow-Up Contacts:

□ _____
□ _____

Customer Contacts:

□ _____
□ _____

Builder Contacts:

□ _____
□ _____

Gratitude:

□ _____

MAY 20TH

□ Supplements □ Water □ Meditate/Mindset □ Movement

To Do List:

□ _____

□ _____

□ _____

□ _____

□ _____

New Prospect Contacts:

□ _____

□ _____

Follow-Up Contacts:

□ _____

□ _____

Customer Contacts:

□ _____

□ _____

Builder Contacts:

□ _____

□ _____

Gratitude:

□ _____

MAY 21ST

□ Supplements   □ Water   □ Meditate/Mindset   □ Movement

To Do List:

□ _____

□ _____

□ _____

□ _____

□ _____

New Prospect Contacts:

□ _____

□ _____

Follow-Up Contacts:

□ _____

□ _____

Customer Contacts:

□ _____

□ _____

Builder Contacts:

□ _____

□ _____

Gratitude:

□ _____

MAY 22ND

☐ Supplements   ☐ Water   ☐ Meditate/Mindset   ☐ Movement

To Do List:

☐ _____

☐ _____

☐ _____

☐ _____

☐ _____

New Prospect Contacts:

☐ _____

☐ _____

Follow-Up Contacts:

☐ _____

☐ _____

Customer Contacts:

☐ _____

☐ _____

Builder Contacts:

☐ _____

☐ _____

Gratitude:

☐ _____

MAY 23RD

☐ Supplements ☐ Water ☐ Meditate/Mindset ☐ Movement

To Do List:

☐ _____

☐ _____

☐ _____

☐ _____

☐ _____

New Prospect Contacts:

☐ _____

☐ _____

Follow-Up Contacts:

☐ _____

☐ _____

Customer Contacts:

☐ _____

☐ _____

Builder Contacts:

☐ _____

☐ _____

Gratitude:

☐ _____

MAY 24TH

☐ Supplements   ☐ Water   ☐ Meditate/Mindset   ☐ Movement

To Do List:

☐ _____

☐ _____

☐ _____

☐ _____

☐ _____

New Prospect Contacts:

☐ _____

☐ _____

Follow-Up Contacts:

☐ _____

☐ _____

Customer Contacts:

☐ _____

☐ _____

Builder Contacts:

☐ _____

☐ _____

Gratitude:

☐ _____

MAY 25TH

□ Supplements   □ Water   □ Meditate/Mindset   □ Movement

To Do List:

□ _____

□ _____

□ _____

□ _____

□ _____

New Prospect Contacts:

□ _____

□ _____

Follow-Up Contacts:

□ _____

□ _____

Customer Contacts:

□ _____

□ _____

Builder Contacts:

□ _____

□ _____

Gratitude:

□ _____

MAY 26TH

☐ Supplements   ☐ Water   ☐ Meditate/Mindset   ☐ Movement

To Do List:

☐ _____

☐ _____

☐ _____

☐ _____

☐ _____

New Prospect Contacts:

☐ _____

☐ _____

Follow-Up Contacts:

☐ _____

☐ _____

Customer Contacts:

☐ _____

☐ _____

Builder Contacts:

☐ _____

☐ _____

Gratitude:

☐ _____

MAY 27TH

☐ Supplements   ☐ Water   ☐ Meditate/Mindset   ☐ Movement

To Do List:

☐ _____

☐ _____

☐ _____

☐ _____

☐ _____

New Prospect Contacts:

☐ _____

☐ _____

Follow-Up Contacts:

☐ _____

☐ _____

Customer Contacts:

☐ _____

☐ _____

Builder Contacts:

☐ _____

☐ _____

Gratitude:

☐ _____

MAY 28TH

□ Supplements   □ Water   □ Meditate/Mindset   □ Movement

To Do List:

□ _____

□ _____

□ _____

□ _____

□ _____

New Prospect Contacts:

□ _____

□ _____

Follow-Up Contacts:

□ _____

□ _____

Customer Contacts:

□ _____

□ _____

Builder Contacts:

□ _____

□ _____

Gratitude:

□ _____

JUNE

JUNE 15TH

☐ Supplements   ☐ Water   ☐ Meditate/Mindset   ☐ Movement

To Do List:

☐ _____

☐ _____

☐ _____

☐ _____

☐ _____

New Prospect Contacts:

☐ _____

☐ _____

Follow-Up Contacts:

☐ _____

☐ _____

Customer Contacts:

☐ _____

☐ _____

Builder Contacts:

☐ _____

☐ _____

Gratitude:

☐ _____

JUNE 16TH

□ Supplements　　□ Water　　□ Meditate/Mindset　　□ Movement

To Do List:

□ _____
□ _____
□ _____
□ _____
□ _____

New Prospect Contacts:

□ _____
□ _____

Follow-Up Contacts:

□ _____
□ _____

Customer Contacts:

□ _____
□ _____

Builder Contacts:

□ _____
□ _____

Gratitude:

□ _____

JUNE 23RD

□ Supplements   □ Water   □ Meditate/Mindset   □ Movement

To Do List:

□ _____
□ _____
□ _____
□ _____
□ _____

New Prospect Contacts:

□ _____
□ _____

Follow-Up Contacts:

□ _____
□ _____

Customer Contacts:

□ _____
□ _____

Builder Contacts:

□ _____
□ _____

Gratitude:

□ _____

JUNE 24TH

To Do List:

☐ _____

☐ _____

☐ _____

☐ _____

☐ _____

New Prospect Contacts:

☐ _____

☐ _____

Follow-Up Contacts:

☐ _____

☐ _____

Customer Contacts:

☐ _____

☐ _____

Builder Contacts:

☐ _____

☐ _____

Gratitude:

☐ _____

JUNE 25TH

☐ Supplements ☐ Water ☐ Meditate/Mindset ☐ Movement

To Do List:

☐ _____

☐ _____

☐ _____

☐ _____

☐ _____

New Prospect Contacts:

☐ _____

☐ _____

Follow-Up Contacts:

☐ _____

☐ _____

Customer Contacts:

☐ _____

☐ _____

Builder Contacts:

☐ _____

☐ _____

Gratitude:

☐ _____

JUNE 26TH

☐ Supplements   ☐ Water   ☐ Meditate/Mindset   ☐ Movement

To Do List:

☐ _____

☐ _____

☐ _____

☐ _____

☐ _____

New Prospect Contacts:

☐ _____

☐ _____

Follow-Up Contacts:

☐ _____

☐ _____

Customer Contacts:

☐ _____

☐ _____

Builder Contacts:

☐ _____

☐ _____

Gratitude:

☐ _____

JUNE 27TH

□ Supplements   □ Water   □ Meditate/Mindset   □ Movement

To Do List:

□ _____

□ _____

□ _____

□ _____

□ _____

New Prospect Contacts:

□ _____

□ _____

Follow-Up Contacts:

□ _____

□ _____

Customer Contacts:

□ _____

□ _____

Builder Contacts:

□ _____

□ _____

Gratitude:

□ _____

JUNE 28TH

☐ Supplements   ☐ Water   ☐ Meditate/Mindset   ☐ Movement

To Do List:

☐ _____

☐ _____

☐ _____

☐ _____

☐ _____

New Prospect Contacts:

☐ _____

☐ _____

Follow-Up Contacts:

☐ _____

☐ _____

Customer Contacts:

☐ _____

☐ _____

Builder Contacts:

☐ _____

☐ _____

Gratitude:

☐ _____

JUNE 29TH

☐ Supplements ☐ Water ☐ Meditate/Mindset ☐ Movement

To Do List:

☐ _____

☐ _____

☐ _____

☐ _____

☐ _____

New Prospect Contacts:

☐ _____

☐ _____

Follow-Up Contacts:

☐ _____

☐ _____

Customer Contacts:

☐ _____

☐ _____

Builder Contacts:

☐ _____

☐ _____

Gratitude:

☐ _____

JUNE 30TH

☐ Supplements   ☐ Water   ☐ Meditate/Mindset   ☐ Movement

To Do List:

☐ _____

☐ _____

☐ _____

☐ _____

☐ _____

New Prospect Contacts:

☐ _____

☐ _____

Follow-Up Contacts:

☐ _____

☐ _____

Customer Contacts:

☐ _____

☐ _____

Builder Contacts:

☐ _____

☐ _____

Gratitude:

☐ _____

JULY

JULY 9TH

☐ Supplements   ☐ Water   ☐ Meditate/Mindset   ☐ Movement

To Do List:

☐ _____

☐ _____

☐ _____

☐ _____

☐ _____

New Prospect Contacts:

☐ _____

☐ _____

Follow-Up Contacts:

☐ _____

☐ _____

Customer Contacts:

☐ _____

☐ _____

Builder Contacts:

☐ _____

☐ _____

Gratitude:

☐ _____

JULY 10TH

☐ Supplements   ☐ Water   ☐ Meditate/Mindset   ☐ Movement

To Do List:

☐ _____

☐ _____

☐ _____

☐ _____

☐ _____

New Prospect Contacts:

☐ _____

☐ _____

Follow-Up Contacts:

☐ _____

☐ _____

Customer Contacts:

☐ _____

☐ _____

Builder Contacts:

☐ _____

☐ _____

Gratitude:

☐ _____

JULY 11TH

□ Supplements   □ Water   □ Meditate/Mindset   □ Movement

To Do List:

□ _____

□ _____

□ _____

□ _____

□ _____

New Prospect Contacts:

□ _____

□ _____

Follow-Up Contacts:

□ _____

□ _____

Customer Contacts:

□ _____

□ _____

Builder Contacts:

□ _____

□ _____

Gratitude:

□ _____

JULY 12TH

☐ Supplements   ☐ Water   ☐ Meditate/Mindset   ☐ Movement

To Do List:

☐ _____

☐ _____

☐ _____

☐ _____

☐ _____

New Prospect Contacts:

☐ _____

☐ _____

Follow-Up Contacts:

☐ _____

☐ _____

Customer Contacts:

☐ _____

☐ _____

Builder Contacts:

☐ _____

☐ _____

Gratitude:

☐ _____

JULY 13TH

☐ Supplements   ☐ Water   ☐ Meditate/Mindset   ☐ Movement

To Do List:

☐ _____

☐ _____

☐ _____

☐ _____

☐ _____

New Prospect Contacts:

☐ _____

☐ _____

Follow-Up Contacts:

☐ _____

☐ _____

Customer Contacts:

☐ _____

☐ _____

Builder Contacts:

☐ _____

☐ _____

Gratitude:

☐ _____

JULY 14TH

☐ Supplements   ☐ Water   ☐ Meditate/Mindset   ☐ Movement

To Do List:

☐ _____

☐ _____

☐ _____

☐ _____

☐ _____

New Prospect Contacts:

☐ _____

☐ _____

Follow-Up Contacts:

☐ _____

☐ _____

Customer Contacts:

☐ _____

☐ _____

Builder Contacts:

☐ _____

☐ _____

Gratitude:

☐ _____

JULY 15TH

□ Supplements   □ Water   □ Meditate/Mindset   □ Movement

To Do List:

□ _____

□ _____

□ _____

□ _____

□ _____

New Prospect Contacts:

□ _____

□ _____

Follow-Up Contacts:

□ _____

□ _____

Customer Contacts:

□ _____

□ _____

Builder Contacts:

□ _____

□ _____

Gratitude:

□ _____

JULY 16TH

□ Supplements   □ Water   □ Meditate/Mindset   □ Movement

To Do List:

□ _____

□ _____

□ _____

□ _____

□ _____

New Prospect Contacts:

□ _____

□ _____

Follow-Up Contacts:

□ _____

□ _____

Customer Contacts:

□ _____

□ _____

Builder Contacts:

□ _____

□ _____

Gratitude:

□ _____

JULY 17TH

☐ Supplements ☐ Water ☐ Meditate/Mindset ☐ Movement

To Do List:

☐ _____

☐ _____

☐ _____

☐ _____

☐ _____

New Prospect Contacts:

☐ _____

☐ _____

Follow-Up Contacts:

☐ _____

☐ _____

Customer Contacts:

☐ _____

☐ _____

Builder Contacts:

☐ _____

☐ _____

Gratitude:

☐ _____

JULY 18TH

☐ Supplements   ☐ Water   ☐ Meditate/Mindset   ☐ Movement

To Do List:

☐ _____
☐ _____
☐ _____
☐ _____
☐ _____

New Prospect Contacts:

☐ _____
☐ _____

Follow-Up Contacts:

☐ _____
☐ _____

Customer Contacts:

☐ _____
☐ _____

Builder Contacts:

☐ _____
☐ _____

Gratitude:

☐ _____

JULY 19TH

□ Supplements   □ Water   □ Meditate/Mindset   □ Movement

To Do List:

- □ _____
- □ _____
- □ _____
- □ _____
- □ _____

New Prospect Contacts:

- □ _____
- □ _____

Follow-Up Contacts:

- □ _____
- □ _____

Customer Contacts:

- □ _____
- □ _____

Builder Contacts:

- □ _____
- □ _____

Gratitude:

- □ _____

JULY 20TH

☐ Supplements ☐ Water ☐ Meditate/Mindset ☐ Movement

To Do List:

☐ _____

☐ _____

☐ _____

☐ _____

☐ _____

New Prospect Contacts:

☐ _____

☐ _____

Follow-Up Contacts:

☐ _____

☐ _____

Customer Contacts:

☐ _____

☐ _____

Builder Contacts:

☐ _____

☐ _____

Gratitude:

☐ _____

JULY 21ST

☐ Supplements   ☐ Water   ☐ Meditate/Mindset   ☐ Movement

To Do List:

☐ _____
☐ _____
☐ _____
☐ _____
☐ _____

New Prospect Contacts:

☐ _____
☐ _____

Follow-Up Contacts:

☐ _____
☐ _____

Customer Contacts:

☐ _____
☐ _____

Builder Contacts:

☐ _____
☐ _____

Gratitude:

☐ _____

JULY 22ND

To Do List:

☐ _____

☐ _____

☐ _____

☐ _____

☐ _____

New Prospect Contacts:

☐ _____

☐ _____

Follow-Up Contacts:

☐ _____

☐ _____

Customer Contacts:

☐ _____

☐ _____

Builder Contacts:

☐ _____

☐ _____

Gratitude:

☐ _____

JULY 23RD

☐ Supplements   ☐ Water   ☐ Meditate/Mindset   ☐ Movement

To Do List:

☐ _____

☐ _____

☐ _____

☐ _____

☐ _____

New Prospect Contacts:

☐ _____

☐ _____

Follow-Up Contacts:

☐ _____

☐ _____

Customer Contacts:

☐ _____

☐ _____

Builder Contacts:

☐ _____

☐ _____

Gratitude:

☐ _____

JULY 24TH

☐ Supplements ☐ Water ☐ Meditate/Mindset ☐ Movement

To Do List:

☐ _____
☐ _____
☐ _____
☐ _____
☐ _____

New Prospect Contacts:

☐ _____
☐ _____

Follow-Up Contacts:

☐ _____
☐ _____

Customer Contacts:

☐ _____
☐ _____

Builder Contacts:

☐ _____
☐ _____

Gratitude:

☐ _____

JULY 25TH

☐ Supplements ☐ Water ☐ Meditate/Mindset ☐ Movement

To Do List:

☐ _____

☐ _____

☐ _____

☐ _____

☐ _____

New Prospect Contacts:

☐ _____

☐ _____

Follow-Up Contacts:

☐ _____

☐ _____

Customer Contacts:

☐ _____

☐ _____

Builder Contacts:

☐ _____

☐ _____

Gratitude:

☐ _____

JULY 26TH

☐ Supplements   ☐ Water   ☐ Meditate/Mindset   ☐ Movement

To Do List:

☐ _____

☐ _____

☐ _____

☐ _____

☐ _____

New Prospect Contacts:

☐ _____

☐ _____

Follow-Up Contacts:

☐ _____

☐ _____

Customer Contacts:

☐ _____

☐ _____

Builder Contacts:

☐ _____

☐ _____

Gratitude:

☐ _____

JULY 27TH

☐ Supplements   ☐ Water   ☐ Meditate/Mindset   ☐ Movement

To Do List:

☐ _____

☐ _____

☐ _____

☐ _____

☐ _____

New Prospect Contacts:

☐ _____

☐ _____

Follow-Up Contacts:

☐ _____

☐ _____

Customer Contacts:

☐ _____

☐ _____

Builder Contacts:

☐ _____

☐ _____

Gratitude:

☐ _____

JULY 28TH

□ Supplements   □ Water   □ Meditate/Mindset   □ Movement

To Do List:

□ _____
□ _____
□ _____
□ _____
□ _____

New Prospect Contacts:

□ _____
□ _____

Follow-Up Contacts:

□ _____
□ _____

Customer Contacts:

□ _____
□ _____

Builder Contacts:

□ _____
□ _____

Gratitude:

□ _____

JULY 29TH

☐ Supplements   ☐ Water   ☐ Meditate/Mindset   ☐ Movement

To Do List:

☐ _____

☐ _____

☐ _____

☐ _____

☐ _____

New Prospect Contacts:

☐ _____

☐ _____

Follow-Up Contacts:

☐ _____

☐ _____

Customer Contacts:

☐ _____

☐ _____

Builder Contacts:

☐ _____

☐ _____

Gratitude:

☐ _____

JULY 30TH

☐ Supplements   ☐ Water   ☐ Meditate/Mindset   ☐ Movement

To Do List:

☐ _____

☐ _____

☐ _____

☐ _____

☐ _____

New Prospect Contacts:

☐ _____

☐ _____

Follow-Up Contacts:

☐ _____

☐ _____

Customer Contacts:

☐ _____

☐ _____

Builder Contacts:

☐ _____

☐ _____

Gratitude:

☐ _____

JULY 31ST

☐ Supplements   ☐ Water   ☐ Meditate/Mindset   ☐ Movement

To Do List:

☐ _____

☐ _____

☐ _____

☐ _____

☐ _____

New Prospect Contacts:

☐ _____

☐ _____

Follow-Up Contacts:

☐ _____

☐ _____

Customer Contacts:

☐ _____

☐ _____

Builder Contacts:

☐ _____

☐ _____

Gratitude:

☐ _____

AUGUST

AUGUST 1ST

☐ Supplements   ☐ Water   ☐ Meditate/Mindset   ☐ Movement

To Do List:

☐ _____

☐ _____

☐ _____

☐ _____

☐ _____

New Prospect Contacts:

☐ _____

☐ _____

Follow-Up Contacts:

☐ _____

☐ _____

Customer Contacts:

☐ _____

☐ _____

Builder Contacts:

☐ _____

☐ _____

Gratitude:

☐ _____

AUGUST 2ND

☐ Supplements   ☐ Water   ☐ Meditate/Mindset   ☐ Movement

To Do List:

☐ _____

☐ _____

☐ _____

☐ _____

☐ _____

New Prospect Contacts:

☐ _____

☐ _____

Follow-Up Contacts:

☐ _____

☐ _____

Customer Contacts:

☐ _____

☐ _____

Builder Contacts:

☐ _____

☐ _____

Gratitude:

☐ _____

AUGUST 3RD

☐ Supplements   ☐ Water   ☐ Meditate/Mindset   ☐ Movement

To Do List:

☐ _____

☐ _____

☐ _____

☐ _____

☐ _____

New Prospect Contacts:

☐ _____

☐ _____

Follow-Up Contacts:

☐ _____

☐ _____

Customer Contacts:

☐ _____

☐ _____

Builder Contacts:

☐ _____

☐ _____

Gratitude:

☐ _____

AUGUST 4TH

To Do List:

- [ ] _____
- [ ] _____
- [ ] _____
- [ ] _____
- [ ] _____

New Prospect Contacts:

- [ ] _____
- [ ] _____

Follow-Up Contacts:

- [ ] _____
- [ ] _____

Customer Contacts:

- [ ] _____
- [ ] _____

Builder Contacts:

- [ ] _____
- [ ] _____

Gratitude:

- [ ] _____

AUGUST 5TH

☐ Supplements   ☐ Water   ☐ Meditate/Mindset   ☐ Movement

To Do List:

☐ _____

☐ _____

☐ _____

☐ _____

☐ _____

New Prospect Contacts:

☐ _____

☐ _____

Follow-Up Contacts:

☐ _____

☐ _____

Customer Contacts:

☐ _____

☐ _____

Builder Contacts:

☐ _____

☐ _____

Gratitude:

☐ _____

AUGUST 6TH

□ Supplements   □ Water   □ Meditate/Mindset   □ Movement

To Do List:

□ _____

□ _____

□ _____

□ _____

□ _____

New Prospect Contacts:

□ _____

□ _____

Follow-Up Contacts:

□ _____

□ _____

Customer Contacts:

□ _____

□ _____

Builder Contacts:

□ _____

□ _____

Gratitude:

□ _____

AUGUST 7TH

☐ Supplements   ☐ Water   ☐ Meditate/Mindset   ☐ Movement

To Do List:

☐ _____

☐ _____

☐ _____

☐ _____

☐ _____

New Prospect Contacts:

☐ _____

☐ _____

Follow-Up Contacts:

☐ _____

☐ _____

Customer Contacts:

☐ _____

☐ _____

Builder Contacts:

☐ _____

☐ _____

Gratitude:

☐ _____

AUGUST 8TH

☐ Supplements ☐ Water ☐ Meditate/Mindset ☐ Movement

To Do List:

☐ _____

☐ _____

☐ _____

☐ _____

☐ _____

New Prospect Contacts:

☐ _____

☐ _____

Follow-Up Contacts:

☐ _____

☐ _____

Customer Contacts:

☐ _____

☐ _____

Builder Contacts:

☐ _____

☐ _____

Gratitude:

☐ _____

AUGUST 9TH

□ Supplements   □ Water   □ Meditate/Mindset   □ Movement

To Do List:

□ _____
□ _____
□ _____
□ _____
□ _____

New Prospect Contacts:

□ _____
□ _____

Follow-Up Contacts:

□ _____
□ _____

Customer Contacts:

□ _____
□ _____

Builder Contacts:

□ _____
□ _____

Gratitude:

□ _____

AUGUST 10TH

□ Supplements   □ Water   □ Meditate/Mindset   □ Movement

To Do List:

□ _____

□ _____

□ _____

□ _____

□ _____

New Prospect Contacts:

□ _____

□ _____

Follow-Up Contacts:

□ _____

□ _____

Customer Contacts:

□ _____

□ _____

Builder Contacts:

□ _____

□ _____

Gratitude:

□ _____

AUGUST 11TH

□ Supplements   □ Water   □ Meditate/Mindset   □ Movement

To Do List:

□ _____

□ _____

□ _____

□ _____

□ _____

New Prospect Contacts:

□ _____

□ _____

Follow-Up Contacts:

□ _____

□ _____

Customer Contacts:

□ _____

□ _____

Builder Contacts:

□ _____

□ _____

Gratitude:

□ _____

AUGUST 12TH

☐ Supplements ☐ Water ☐ Meditate/Mindset ☐ Movement

To Do List:

☐ _____

☐ _____

☐ _____

☐ _____

☐ _____

New Prospect Contacts:

☐ _____

☐ _____

Follow-Up Contacts:

☐ _____

☐ _____

Customer Contacts:

☐ _____

☐ _____

Builder Contacts:

☐ _____

☐ _____

Gratitude:

☐ _____

AUGUST 13TH

□ Supplements   □ Water   □ Meditate/Mindset   □ Movement

To Do List:

□ _____

□ _____

□ _____

□ _____

□ _____

New Prospect Contacts:

□ _____

□ _____

Follow-Up Contacts:

□ _____

□ _____

Customer Contacts:

□ _____

□ _____

Builder Contacts:

□ _____

□ _____

Gratitude:

□ _____

AUGUST 14TH

☐ Supplements   ☐ Water   ☐ Meditate/Mindset   ☐ Movement

To Do List:

☐ _____

☐ _____

☐ _____

☐ _____

☐ _____

New Prospect Contacts:

☐ _____

☐ _____

Follow-Up Contacts:

☐ _____

☐ _____

Customer Contacts:

☐ _____

☐ _____

Builder Contacts:

☐ _____

☐ _____

Gratitude:

☐ _____

AUGUST 15TH

☐ Supplements ☐ Water ☐ Meditate/Mindset ☐ Movement

To Do List:

☐ _____

☐ _____

☐ _____

☐ _____

☐ _____

New Prospect Contacts:

☐ _____

☐ _____

Follow-Up Contacts:

☐ _____

☐ _____

Customer Contacts:

☐ _____

☐ _____

Builder Contacts:

☐ _____

☐ _____

Gratitude:

☐ _____

AUGUST 16TH

☐ Supplements   ☐ Water   ☐ Meditate/Mindset   ☐ Movement

To Do List:

☐ _____

☐ _____

☐ _____

☐ _____

☐ _____

New Prospect Contacts:

☐ _____

☐ _____

Follow-Up Contacts:

☐ _____

☐ _____

Customer Contacts:

☐ _____

☐ _____

Builder Contacts:

☐ _____

☐ _____

Gratitude:

☐ _____

AUGUST 17TH

□ Supplements   □ Water   □ Meditate/Mindset   □ Movement

To Do List:

□ _____

□ _____

□ _____

□ _____

□ _____

New Prospect Contacts:

□ _____

□ _____

Follow-Up Contacts:

□ _____

□ _____

Customer Contacts:

□ _____

□ _____

Builder Contacts:

□ _____

□ _____

Gratitude:

□ _____

AUGUST 18TH

☐ Supplements   ☐ Water   ☐ Meditate/Mindset   ☐ Movement

To Do List:

☐ _____

☐ _____

☐ _____

☐ _____

☐ _____

New Prospect Contacts:

☐ _____

☐ _____

Follow-Up Contacts:

☐ _____

☐ _____

Customer Contacts:

☐ _____

☐ _____

Builder Contacts:

☐ _____

☐ _____

Gratitude:

☐ _____

AUGUST 19TH

☐ Supplements   ☐ Water   ☐ Meditate/Mindset   ☐ Movement

To Do List:

☐ _____

☐ _____

☐ _____

☐ _____

☐ _____

New Prospect Contacts:

☐ _____

☐ _____

Follow-Up Contacts:

☐ _____

☐ _____

Customer Contacts:

☐ _____

☐ _____

Builder Contacts:

☐ _____

☐ _____

Gratitude:

☐ _____

AUGUST 20TH

□ Supplements   □ Water   □ Meditate/Mindset   □ Movement

To Do List:

□ _____

□ _____

□ _____

□ _____

□ _____

New Prospect Contacts:

□ _____

□ _____

Follow-Up Contacts:

□ _____

□ _____

Customer Contacts:

□ _____

□ _____

Builder Contacts:

□ _____

□ _____

Gratitude:

□ _____

AUGUST 21ST

To Do List:

□ _____

□ _____

□ _____

□ _____

□ _____

New Prospect Contacts:

□ _____

□ _____

Follow-Up Contacts:

□ _____

□ _____

Customer Contacts:

□ _____

□ _____

Builder Contacts:

□ _____

□ _____

Gratitude:

□ _____

AUGUST 22ND

□ Supplements   □ Water   □ Meditate/Mindset   □ Movement

To Do List:

□ _____

□ _____

□ _____

□ _____

□ _____

New Prospect Contacts:

□ _____

□ _____

Follow-Up Contacts:

□ _____

□ _____

Customer Contacts:

□ _____

□ _____

Builder Contacts:

□ _____

□ _____

Gratitude:

□ _____

AUGUST 23RD

☐ Supplements   ☐ Water   ☐ Meditate/Mindset   ☐ Movement

To Do List:

☐ _____

☐ _____

☐ _____

☐ _____

☐ _____

New Prospect Contacts:

☐ _____

☐ _____

Follow-Up Contacts:

☐ _____

☐ _____

Customer Contacts:

☐ _____

☐ _____

Builder Contacts:

☐ _____

☐ _____

Gratitude:

☐ _____

AUGUST 24TH

☐ Supplements   ☐ Water   ☐ Meditate/Mindset   ☐ Movement

To Do List:

☐ _____

☐ _____

☐ _____

☐ _____

☐ _____

New Prospect Contacts:

☐ _____

☐ _____

Follow-Up Contacts:

☐ _____

☐ _____

Customer Contacts:

☐ _____

☐ _____

Builder Contacts:

☐ _____

☐ _____

Gratitude:

☐ _____

AUGUST 25TH

□ Supplements   □ Water   □ Meditate/Mindset   □ Movement

To Do List:

□ _____

□ _____

□ _____

□ _____

□ _____

New Prospect Contacts:

□ _____

□ _____

Follow-Up Contacts:

□ _____

□ _____

Customer Contacts:

□ _____

□ _____

Builder Contacts:

□ _____

□ _____

Gratitude:

□ _____

AUGUST 26TH

☐ Supplements   ☐ Water   ☐ Meditate/Mindset   ☐ Movement

To Do List:

☐ _____

☐ _____

☐ _____

☐ _____

☐ _____

New Prospect Contacts:

☐ _____

☐ _____

Follow-Up Contacts:

☐ _____

☐ _____

Customer Contacts:

☐ _____

☐ _____

Builder Contacts:

☐ _____

☐ _____

Gratitude:

☐ _____

AUGUST 27TH

☐ Supplements   ☐ Water   ☐ Meditate/Mindset   ☐ Movement

To Do List:

☐ _____
☐ _____
☐ _____
☐ _____
☐ _____

New Prospect Contacts:

☐ _____
☐ _____

Follow-Up Contacts:

☐ _____
☐ _____

Customer Contacts:

☐ _____
☐ _____

Builder Contacts:

☐ _____
☐ _____

Gratitude:

☐ _____

AUGUST 28TH

☐ Supplements   ☐ Water   ☐ Meditate/Mindset   ☐ Movement

To Do List:

☐ _____

☐ _____

☐ _____

☐ _____

☐ _____

New Prospect Contacts:

☐ _____

☐ _____

Follow-Up Contacts:

☐ _____

☐ _____

Customer Contacts:

☐ _____

☐ _____

Builder Contacts:

☐ _____

☐ _____

Gratitude:

☐ _____

AUGUST 29TH

□ Supplements   □ Water   □ Meditate/Mindset   □ Movement

To Do List:

□ _____

□ _____

□ _____

□ _____

□ _____

New Prospect Contacts:

□ _____

□ _____

Follow-Up Contacts:

□ _____

□ _____

Customer Contacts:

□ _____

□ _____

Builder Contacts:

□ _____

□ _____

Gratitude:

□ _____

AUGUST 30TH

□ Supplements □ Water □ Meditate/Mindset □ Movement

To Do List:

□ _____
□ _____
□ _____
□ _____
□ _____

New Prospect Contacts:

□ _____
□ _____

Follow-Up Contacts:

□ _____
□ _____

Customer Contacts:

□ _____
□ _____

Builder Contacts:

□ _____
□ _____

Gratitude:

□ _____

AUGUST 31ST

☐ Supplements   ☐ Water   ☐ Meditate/Mindset   ☐ Movement

To Do List:

☐ _____

☐ _____

☐ _____

☐ _____

☐ _____

New Prospect Contacts:

☐ _____

☐ _____

Follow-Up Contacts:

☐ _____

☐ _____

Customer Contacts:

☐ _____

☐ _____

Builder Contacts:

☐ _____

☐ _____

Gratitude:

☐ _____

SEPTEMBER

SEPTEMBER 1ST

□ Supplements   □ Water   □ Meditate/Mindset   □ Movement

To Do List:

□ _____

□ _____

□ _____

□ _____

□ _____

New Prospect Contacts:

□ _____

□ _____

Follow-Up Contacts:

□ _____

□ _____

Customer Contacts:

□ _____

□ _____

Builder Contacts:

□ _____

□ _____

Gratitude:

□ _____

SEPTEMBER 2ND

□ Supplements   □ Water   □ Meditate/Mindset   □ Movement

To Do List:

□ _____

□ _____

□ _____

□ _____

□ _____

New Prospect Contacts:

□ _____

□ _____

Follow-Up Contacts:

□ _____

□ _____

Customer Contacts:

□ _____

□ _____

Builder Contacts:

□ _____

□ _____

Gratitude:

□ _____

SEPTEMBER 3RD

☐ Supplements   ☐ Water   ☐ Meditate/Mindset   ☐ Movement

To Do List:

☐ _____
☐ _____
☐ _____
☐ _____
☐ _____

New Prospect Contacts:

☐ _____
☐ _____

Follow-Up Contacts:

☐ _____
☐ _____

Customer Contacts:

☐ _____
☐ _____

Builder Contacts:

☐ _____
☐ _____

Gratitude:

☐ _____

SEPTEMBER 4TH

□ Supplements   □ Water   □ Meditate/Mindset   □ Movement

To Do List:

□ _____

□ _____

□ _____

□ _____

□ _____

New Prospect Contacts:

□ _____

□ _____

Follow-Up Contacts:

□ _____

□ _____

Customer Contacts:

□ _____

□ _____

Builder Contacts:

□ _____

□ _____

Gratitude:

□ _____

SEPTEMBER 5TH

☐ Supplements ☐ Water ☐ Meditate/Mindset ☐ Movement

To Do List:

☐ _____

☐ _____

☐ _____

☐ _____

☐ _____

New Prospect Contacts:

☐ _____

☐ _____

Follow-Up Contacts:

☐ _____

☐ _____

Customer Contacts:

☐ _____

☐ _____

Builder Contacts:

☐ _____

☐ _____

Gratitude:

☐ _____

SEPTEMBER 6TH

☐ Supplements ☐ Water ☐ Meditate/Mindset ☐ Movement

To Do List:

☐ _____

☐ _____

☐ _____

☐ _____

☐ _____

New Prospect Contacts:

☐ _____

☐ _____

Follow-Up Contacts:

☐ _____

☐ _____

Customer Contacts:

☐ _____

☐ _____

Builder Contacts:

☐ _____

☐ _____

Gratitude:

☐ _____

SEPTEMBER 7TH

☐ Supplements   ☐ Water   ☐ Meditate/Mindset   ☐ Movement

To Do List:

☐ _____

☐ _____

☐ _____

☐ _____

☐ _____

New Prospect Contacts:

☐ _____

☐ _____

Follow-Up Contacts:

☐ _____

☐ _____

Customer Contacts:

☐ _____

☐ _____

Builder Contacts:

☐ _____

☐ _____

Gratitude:

☐ _____

SEPTEMBER 8TH

☐ Supplements   ☐ Water   ☐ Meditate/Mindset   ☐ Movement

To Do List:

☐ _____
☐ _____
☐ _____
☐ _____
☐ _____

New Prospect Contacts:

☐ _____
☐ _____

Follow-Up Contacts:

☐ _____
☐ _____

Customer Contacts:

☐ _____
☐ _____

Builder Contacts:

☐ _____
☐ _____

Gratitude:

☐ _____

SEPTEMBER 9TH

☐ Supplements   ☐ Water   ☐ Meditate/Mindset   ☐ Movement

To Do List:

☐ _____

☐ _____

☐ _____

☐ _____

☐ _____

New Prospect Contacts:

☐ _____

☐ _____

Follow-Up Contacts:

☐ _____

☐ _____

Customer Contacts:

☐ _____

☐ _____

Builder Contacts:

☐ _____

☐ _____

Gratitude:

☐ _____

SEPTEMBER 10TH

☐ Supplements   ☐ Water   ☐ Meditate/Mindset   ☐ Movement

To Do List:

☐ _____

☐ _____

☐ _____

☐ _____

☐ _____

New Prospect Contacts:

☐ _____

☐ _____

Follow-Up Contacts:

☐ _____

☐ _____

Customer Contacts:

☐ _____

☐ _____

Builder Contacts:

☐ _____

☐ _____

Gratitude:

☐ _____

SEPTEMBER 11TH

□ Supplements   □ Water   □ Meditate/Mindset   □ Movement

To Do List:

□ _____

□ _____

□ _____

□ _____

□ _____

New Prospect Contacts:

□ _____

□ _____

Follow-Up Contacts:

□ _____

□ _____

Customer Contacts:

□ _____

□ _____

Builder Contacts:

□ _____

□ _____

Gratitude:

□ _____

SEPTEMBER 12TH

□ Supplements   □ Water   □ Meditate/Mindset   □ Movement

To Do List:

□ _____

□ _____

□ _____

□ _____

□ _____

New Prospect Contacts:

□ _____

□ _____

Follow-Up Contacts:

□ _____

□ _____

Customer Contacts:

□ _____

□ _____

Builder Contacts:

□ _____

□ _____

Gratitude:

□ _____

SEPTEMBER 13TH

☐ Supplements   ☐ Water   ☐ Meditate/Mindset   ☐ Movement

To Do List:

☐ _____

☐ _____

☐ _____

☐ _____

☐ _____

New Prospect Contacts:

☐ _____

☐ _____

Follow-Up Contacts:

☐ _____

☐ _____

Customer Contacts:

☐ _____

☐ _____

Builder Contacts:

☐ _____

☐ _____

Gratitude:

☐ _____

SEPTEMBER 14TH

☐ Supplements   ☐ Water   ☐ Meditate/Mindset   ☐ Movement

To Do List:

☐ _____

☐ _____

☐ _____

☐ _____

☐ _____

New Prospect Contacts:

☐ _____

☐ _____

Follow-Up Contacts:

☐ _____

☐ _____

Customer Contacts:

☐ _____

☐ _____

Builder Contacts:

☐ _____

☐ _____

Gratitude:

☐ _____

SEPTEMBER 15TH

☐ Supplements   ☐ Water   ☐ Meditate/Mindset   ☐ Movement

To Do List:

☐ _____

☐ _____

☐ _____

☐ _____

☐ _____

New Prospect Contacts:

☐ _____

☐ _____

Follow-Up Contacts:

☐ _____

☐ _____

Customer Contacts:

☐ _____

☐ _____

Builder Contacts:

☐ _____

☐ _____

Gratitude:

☐ _____

SEPTEMBER 16TH

☐ Supplements   ☐ Water   ☐ Meditate/Mindset   ☐ Movement

To Do List:

☐ _____

☐ _____

☐ _____

☐ _____

☐ _____

New Prospect Contacts:

☐ _____

☐ _____

Follow-Up Contacts:

☐ _____

☐ _____

Customer Contacts:

☐ _____

☐ _____

Builder Contacts:

☐ _____

☐ _____

Gratitude:

☐ _____

SEPTEMBER 17TH

□ Supplements   □ Water   □ Meditate/Mindset   □ Movement

To Do List:

□ _____

□ _____

□ _____

□ _____

□ _____

New Prospect Contacts:

□ _____

□ _____

Follow-Up Contacts:

□ _____

□ _____

Customer Contacts:

□ _____

□ _____

Builder Contacts:

□ _____

□ _____

Gratitude:

□ _____

SEPTEMBER 18TH

☐ Supplements   ☐ Water   ☐ Meditate/Mindset   ☐ Movement

To Do List:

☐ _____

☐ _____

☐ _____

☐ _____

☐ _____

New Prospect Contacts:

☐ _____

☐ _____

Follow-Up Contacts:

☐ _____

☐ _____

Customer Contacts:

☐ _____

☐ _____

Builder Contacts:

☐ _____

☐ _____

Gratitude:

☐ _____

SEPTEMBER 19TH

□ Supplements   □ Water   □ Meditate/Mindset   □ Movement

To Do List:

□ _____

□ _____

□ _____

□ _____

□ _____

New Prospect Contacts:

□ _____

□ _____

Follow-Up Contacts:

□ _____

□ _____

Customer Contacts:

□ _____

□ _____

Builder Contacts:

□ _____

□ _____

Gratitude:

□ _____

SEPTEMBER 20TH

☐ Supplements   ☐ Water   ☐ Meditate/Mindset   ☐ Movement

To Do List:

☐ _____

☐ _____

☐ _____

☐ _____

☐ _____

New Prospect Contacts:

☐ _____

☐ _____

Follow-Up Contacts:

☐ _____

☐ _____

Customer Contacts:

☐ _____

☐ _____

Builder Contacts:

☐ _____

☐ _____

Gratitude:

☐ _____

SEPTEMBER 21ST

☐ Supplements   ☐ Water   ☐ Meditate/Mindset   ☐ Movement

To Do List:

☐ _____

☐ _____

☐ _____

☐ _____

☐ _____

New Prospect Contacts:

☐ _____

☐ _____

Follow-Up Contacts:

☐ _____

☐ _____

Customer Contacts:

☐ _____

☐ _____

Builder Contacts:

☐ _____

☐ _____

Gratitude:

☐ _____

SEPTEMBER 22ND

☐ Supplements   ☐ Water   ☐ Meditate/Mindset   ☐ Movement

To Do List:

☐ _____

☐ _____

☐ _____

☐ _____

☐ _____

New Prospect Contacts:

☐ _____

☐ _____

Follow-Up Contacts:

☐ _____

☐ _____

Customer Contacts:

☐ _____

☐ _____

Builder Contacts:

☐ _____

☐ _____

Gratitude:

☐ _____

SEPTEMBER 23RD

☐ Supplements   ☐ Water   ☐ Meditate/Mindset   ☐ Movement

To Do List:

☐ _____

☐ _____

☐ _____

☐ _____

☐ _____

New Prospect Contacts:

☐ _____

☐ _____

Follow-Up Contacts:

☐ _____

☐ _____

Customer Contacts:

☐ _____

☐ _____

Builder Contacts:

☐ _____

☐ _____

Gratitude:

☐ _____

SEPTEMBER 24TH

☐ Supplements ☐ Water ☐ Meditate/Mindset ☐ Movement

To Do List:

☐ _____

☐ _____

☐ _____

☐ _____

☐ _____

New Prospect Contacts:

☐ _____

☐ _____

Follow-Up Contacts:

☐ _____

☐ _____

Customer Contacts:

☐ _____

☐ _____

Builder Contacts:

☐ _____

☐ _____

Gratitude:

☐ _____

SEPTEMBER 25TH

☐ Supplements   ☐ Water   ☐ Meditate/Mindset   ☐ Movement

To Do List:

☐ _____

☐ _____

☐ _____

☐ _____

☐ _____

New Prospect Contacts:

☐ _____

☐ _____

Follow-Up Contacts:

☐ _____

☐ _____

Customer Contacts:

☐ _____

☐ _____

Builder Contacts:

☐ _____

☐ _____

Gratitude:

☐ _____

SEPTEMBER 26TH

☐ Supplements   ☐ Water   ☐ Meditate/Mindset   ☐ Movement

To Do List:

☐ _____

☐ _____

☐ _____

☐ _____

☐ _____

New Prospect Contacts:

☐ _____

☐ _____

Follow-Up Contacts:

☐ _____

☐ _____

Customer Contacts:

☐ _____

☐ _____

Builder Contacts:

☐ _____

☐ _____

Gratitude:

☐ _____

SEPTEMBER 27TH

☐ Supplements ☐ Water ☐ Meditate/Mindset ☐ Movement

To Do List:

☐ _____
☐ _____
☐ _____
☐ _____
☐ _____

New Prospect Contacts:

☐ _____
☐ _____

Follow-Up Contacts:

☐ _____
☐ _____

Customer Contacts:

☐ _____
☐ _____

Builder Contacts:

☐ _____
☐ _____

Gratitude:

☐ _____

SEPTEMBER 28TH

☐ Supplements   ☐ Water   ☐ Meditate/Mindset   ☐ Movement

To Do List:

☐ _____

☐ _____

☐ _____

☐ _____

☐ _____

New Prospect Contacts:

☐ _____

☐ _____

Follow-Up Contacts:

☐ _____

☐ _____

Customer Contacts:

☐ _____

☐ _____

Builder Contacts:

☐ _____

☐ _____

Gratitude:

☐ _____

SEPTEMBER 29TH

☐ Supplements ☐ Water ☐ Meditate/Mindset ☐ Movement

To Do List:

☐ _____

☐ _____

☐ _____

☐ _____

☐ _____

New Prospect Contacts:

☐ _____

☐ _____

Follow-Up Contacts:

☐ _____

☐ _____

Customer Contacts:

☐ _____

☐ _____

Builder Contacts:

☐ _____

☐ _____

Gratitude:

☐ _____

SEPTEMBER 30TH

☐ Supplements   ☐ Water   ☐ Meditate/Mindset   ☐ Movement

To Do List:

☐ _____

☐ _____

☐ _____

☐ _____

☐ _____

New Prospect Contacts:

☐ _____

☐ _____

Follow-Up Contacts:

☐ _____

☐ _____

Customer Contacts:

☐ _____

☐ _____

Builder Contacts:

☐ _____

☐ _____

Gratitude:

☐ _____

OCTOBER

OCTOBER 1ST

□ Supplements   □ Water   □ Meditate/Mindset   □ Movement

To Do List:

□ _____

□ _____

□ _____

□ _____

□ _____

New Prospect Contacts:

□ _____

□ _____

Follow-Up Contacts:

□ _____

□ _____

Customer Contacts:

□ _____

□ _____

Builder Contacts:

□ _____

□ _____

Gratitude:

□ _____

OCTOBER 2ND

☐ Supplements   ☐ Water   ☐ Meditate/Mindset   ☐ Movement

To Do List:

☐ _____

☐ _____

☐ _____

☐ _____

☐ _____

New Prospect Contacts:

☐ _____

☐ _____

Follow-Up Contacts:

☐ _____

☐ _____

Customer Contacts:

☐ _____

☐ _____

Builder Contacts:

☐ _____

☐ _____

Gratitude:

☐ _____

OCTOBER 3RD

□ Supplements   □ Water   □ Meditate/Mindset   □ Movement

To Do List:

□ _____
□ _____
□ _____
□ _____
□ _____

New Prospect Contacts:

□ _____
□ _____

Follow-Up Contacts:

□ _____
□ _____

Customer Contacts:

□ _____
□ _____

Builder Contacts:

□ _____
□ _____

Gratitude:

□ _____

OCTOBER 4TH

□ Supplements   □ Water   □ Meditate/Mindset   □ Movement

To Do List:

□ _____

□ _____

□ _____

□ _____

□ _____

New Prospect Contacts:

□ _____

□ _____

Follow-Up Contacts:

□ _____

□ _____

Customer Contacts:

□ _____

□ _____

Builder Contacts:

□ _____

□ _____

Gratitude:

□ _____

OCTOBER 5TH

☐ Supplements ☐ Water ☐ Meditate/Mindset ☐ Movement

To Do List:

☐ _____

☐ _____

☐ _____

☐ _____

☐ _____

New Prospect Contacts:

☐ _____

☐ _____

Follow-Up Contacts:

☐ _____

☐ _____

Customer Contacts:

☐ _____

☐ _____

Builder Contacts:

☐ _____

☐ _____

Gratitude:

☐ _____

OCTOBER 6TH

□ Supplements □ Water □ Meditate/Mindset □ Movement

To Do List:

□ _____

□ _____

□ _____

□ _____

□ _____

New Prospect Contacts:

□ _____

□ _____

Follow-Up Contacts:

□ _____

□ _____

Customer Contacts:

□ _____

□ _____

Builder Contacts:

□ _____

□ _____

Gratitude:

□ _____

OCTOBER 7TH

To Do List:

- ☐ _____
- ☐ _____
- ☐ _____
- ☐ _____
- ☐ _____

New Prospect Contacts:

- ☐ _____
- ☐ _____

Follow-Up Contacts:

- ☐ _____
- ☐ _____

Customer Contacts:

- ☐ _____
- ☐ _____

Builder Contacts:

- ☐ _____
- ☐ _____

Gratitude:

- ☐ _____

OCTOBER 8TH

□ Supplements   □ Water   □ Meditate/Mindset   □ Movement

To Do List:

□ _____
□ _____
□ _____
□ _____
□ _____

New Prospect Contacts:

□ _____
□ _____

Follow-Up Contacts:

□ _____
□ _____

Customer Contacts:

□ _____
□ _____

Builder Contacts:

□ _____
□ _____

Gratitude:

□ _____

OCTOBER 9TH

□ Supplements   □ Water   □ Meditate/Mindset   □ Movement

To Do List:

□ _____

□ _____

□ _____

□ _____

□ _____

New Prospect Contacts:

□ _____

□ _____

Follow-Up Contacts:

□ _____

□ _____

Customer Contacts:

□ _____

□ _____

Builder Contacts:

□ _____

□ _____

Gratitude:

□ _____

OCTOBER 10TH

□ Supplements   □ Water   □ Meditate/Mindset   □ Movement

To Do List:

□ _____

□ _____

□ _____

□ _____

□ _____

New Prospect Contacts:

□ _____

□ _____

Follow-Up Contacts:

□ _____

□ _____

Customer Contacts:

□ _____

□ _____

Builder Contacts:

□ _____

□ _____

Gratitude:

□ _____

OCTOBER 11TH

☐ Supplements   ☐ Water   ☐ Meditate/Mindset   ☐ Movement

To Do List:

☐ _____

☐ _____

☐ _____

☐ _____

☐ _____

New Prospect Contacts:

☐ _____

☐ _____

Follow-Up Contacts:

☐ _____

☐ _____

Customer Contacts:

☐ _____

☐ _____

Builder Contacts:

☐ _____

☐ _____

Gratitude:

☐ _____

OCTOBER 12TH

□ Supplements   □ Water   □ Meditate/Mindset   □ Movement

To Do List:

□ _____

□ _____

□ _____

□ _____

□ _____

New Prospect Contacts:

□ _____

□ _____

Follow-Up Contacts:

□ _____

□ _____

Customer Contacts:

□ _____

□ _____

Builder Contacts:

□ _____

□ _____

Gratitude:

□ _____

OCTOBER 13TH

☐ Supplements   ☐ Water   ☐ Meditate/Mindset   ☐ Movement

To Do List:

☐ _____

☐ _____

☐ _____

☐ _____

☐ _____

New Prospect Contacts:

☐ _____

☐ _____

Follow-Up Contacts:

☐ _____

☐ _____

Customer Contacts:

☐ _____

☐ _____

Builder Contacts:

☐ _____

☐ _____

Gratitude:

☐ _____

OCTOBER 14TH

☐ Supplements   ☐ Water   ☐ Meditate/Mindset   ☐ Movement

To Do List:

☐ _____

☐ _____

☐ _____

☐ _____

☐ _____

New Prospect Contacts:

☐ _____

☐ _____

Follow-Up Contacts:

☐ _____

☐ _____

Customer Contacts:

☐ _____

☐ _____

Builder Contacts:

☐ _____

☐ _____

Gratitude:

☐ _____

OCTOBER 15TH

□ Supplements   □ Water   □ Meditate/Mindset   □ Movement

To Do List:

□ _____

□ _____

□ _____

□ _____

□ _____

New Prospect Contacts:

□ _____

□ _____

Follow-Up Contacts:

□ _____

□ _____

Customer Contacts:

□ _____

□ _____

Builder Contacts:

□ _____

□ _____

Gratitude:

□ _____

OCTOBER 16TH

□ Supplements   □ Water   □ Meditate/Mindset   □ Movement

To Do List:

□ _____

□ _____

□ _____

□ _____

□ _____

New Prospect Contacts:

□ _____

□ _____

Follow-Up Contacts:

□ _____

□ _____

Customer Contacts:

□ _____

□ _____

Builder Contacts:

□ _____

□ _____

Gratitude:

□ _____

OCTOBER 17TH

☐ Supplements ☐ Water ☐ Meditate/Mindset ☐ Movement

To Do List:

☐ _____

☐ _____

☐ _____

☐ _____

☐ _____

New Prospect Contacts:

☐ _____

☐ _____

Follow-Up Contacts:

☐ _____

☐ _____

Customer Contacts:

☐ _____

☐ _____

Builder Contacts:

☐ _____

☐ _____

Gratitude:

☐ _____

OCTOBER 18TH

□ Supplements   □ Water   □ Meditate/Mindset   □ Movement

To Do List:

□ _____

□ _____

□ _____

□ _____

□ _____

New Prospect Contacts:

□ _____

□ _____

Follow-Up Contacts:

□ _____

□ _____

Customer Contacts:

□ _____

□ _____

Builder Contacts:

□ _____

□ _____

Gratitude:

□ _____

OCTOBER 19TH

☐ Supplements   ☐ Water   ☐ Meditate/Mindset   ☐ Movement

To Do List:

☐ _____

☐ _____

☐ _____

☐ _____

☐ _____

New Prospect Contacts:

☐ _____

☐ _____

Follow-Up Contacts:

☐ _____

☐ _____

Customer Contacts:

☐ _____

☐ _____

Builder Contacts:

☐ _____

☐ _____

Gratitude:

☐ _____

OCTOBER 20TH

To Do List:

□ _____

□ _____

□ _____

□ _____

□ _____

New Prospect Contacts:

□ _____

□ _____

Follow-Up Contacts:

□ _____

□ _____

Customer Contacts:

□ _____

□ _____

Builder Contacts:

□ _____

□ _____

Gratitude:

□ _____

OCTOBER 21ST

☐ Supplements   ☐ Water   ☐ Meditate/Mindset   ☐ Movement

To Do List:

☐ _____

☐ _____

☐ _____

☐ _____

☐ _____

New Prospect Contacts:

☐ _____

☐ _____

Follow-Up Contacts:

☐ _____

☐ _____

Customer Contacts:

☐ _____

☐ _____

Builder Contacts:

☐ _____

☐ _____

Gratitude:

☐ _____

OCTOBER 22ND

□ Supplements □ Water □ Meditate/Mindset □ Movement

To Do List:

□ _____

□ _____

□ _____

□ _____

□ _____

New Prospect Contacts:

□ _____

□ _____

Follow-Up Contacts:

□ _____

□ _____

Customer Contacts:

□ _____

□ _____

Builder Contacts:

□ _____

□ _____

Gratitude:

□ _____

OCTOBER 23RD

☐ Supplements   ☐ Water   ☐ Meditate/Mindset   ☐ Movement

To Do List:

☐ _____

☐ _____

☐ _____

☐ _____

☐ _____

New Prospect Contacts:

☐ _____

☐ _____

Follow-Up Contacts:

☐ _____

☐ _____

Customer Contacts:

☐ _____

☐ _____

Builder Contacts:

☐ _____

☐ _____

Gratitude:

☐ _____

OCTOBER 24TH

To Do List:

☐ _____

☐ _____

☐ _____

☐ _____

☐ _____

New Prospect Contacts:

☐ _____

☐ _____

Follow-Up Contacts:

☐ _____

☐ _____

Customer Contacts:

☐ _____

☐ _____

Builder Contacts:

☐ _____

☐ _____

Gratitude:

☐ _____

OCTOBER 25TH

☐ Supplements   ☐ Water   ☐ Meditate/Mindset   ☐ Movement

To Do List:

☐ _____

☐ _____

☐ _____

☐ _____

☐ _____

New Prospect Contacts:

☐ _____

☐ _____

Follow-Up Contacts:

☐ _____

☐ _____

Customer Contacts:

☐ _____

☐ _____

Builder Contacts:

☐ _____

☐ _____

Gratitude:

☐ _____

OCTOBER 26TH

☐ Supplements   ☐ Water   ☐ Meditate/Mindset   ☐ Movement

To Do List:

☐ _____

☐ _____

☐ _____

☐ _____

☐ _____

New Prospect Contacts:

☐ _____

☐ _____

Follow-Up Contacts:

☐ _____

☐ _____

Customer Contacts:

☐ _____

☐ _____

Builder Contacts:

☐ _____

☐ _____

Gratitude:

☐ _____

OCTOBER 27TH

☐ Supplements ☐ Water ☐ Meditate/Mindset ☐ Movement

To Do List:

☐ _____

☐ _____

☐ _____

☐ _____

☐ _____

New Prospect Contacts:

☐ _____

☐ _____

Follow-Up Contacts:

☐ _____

☐ _____

Customer Contacts:

☐ _____

☐ _____

Builder Contacts:

☐ _____

☐ _____

Gratitude:

☐ _____

OCTOBER 28TH

☐ Supplements   ☐ Water   ☐ Meditate/Mindset   ☐ Movement

To Do List:

☐ _____

☐ _____

☐ _____

☐ _____

☐ _____

New Prospect Contacts:

☐ _____

☐ _____

Follow-Up Contacts:

☐ _____

☐ _____

Customer Contacts:

☐ _____

☐ _____

Builder Contacts:

☐ _____

☐ _____

Gratitude:

☐ _____

OCTOBER 29TH

☐ Supplements   ☐ Water   ☐ Meditate/Mindset   ☐ Movement

To Do List:

☐ _____

☐ _____

☐ _____

☐ _____

☐ _____

New Prospect Contacts:

☐ _____

☐ _____

Follow-Up Contacts:

☐ _____

☐ _____

Customer Contacts:

☐ _____

☐ _____

Builder Contacts:

☐ _____

☐ _____

Gratitude:

☐ _____

OCTOBER 30TH

☐ Supplements   ☐ Water   ☐ Meditate/Mindset   ☐ Movement

To Do List:

☐ _____

☐ _____

☐ _____

☐ _____

☐ _____

New Prospect Contacts:

☐ _____

☐ _____

Follow-Up Contacts:

☐ _____

☐ _____

Customer Contacts:

☐ _____

☐ _____

Builder Contacts:

☐ _____

☐ _____

Gratitude:

☐ _____

OCTOBER 31ST

□ Supplements □ Water □ Meditate/Mindset □ Movement

To Do List:

□ _____

□ _____

□ _____

□ _____

□ _____

New Prospect Contacts:

□ _____

□ _____

Follow-Up Contacts:

□ _____

□ _____

Customer Contacts:

□ _____

□ _____

Builder Contacts:

□ _____

□ _____

Gratitude:

□ _____

NOVEMBER

NOVEMBER 1ST

☐ Supplements   ☐ Water   ☐ Meditate/Mindset   ☐ Movement

To Do List:

☐ _____

☐ _____

☐ _____

☐ _____

☐ _____

New Prospect Contacts:

☐ _____

☐ _____

Follow-Up Contacts:

☐ _____

☐ _____

Customer Contacts:

☐ _____

☐ _____

Builder Contacts:

☐ _____

☐ _____

Gratitude:

☐ _____

NOVEMBER 2ND

☐ Supplements   ☐ Water   ☐ Meditate/Mindset   ☐ Movement

To Do List:

☐ _____

☐ _____

☐ _____

☐ _____

☐ _____

New Prospect Contacts:

☐ _____

☐ _____

Follow-Up Contacts:

☐ _____

☐ _____

Customer Contacts:

☐ _____

☐ _____

Builder Contacts:

☐ _____

☐ _____

Gratitude:

☐ _____

NOVEMBER 3RD

☐ Supplements   ☐ Water   ☐ Meditate/Mindset   ☐ Movement

To Do List:

☐ _____

☐ _____

☐ _____

☐ _____

☐ _____

New Prospect Contacts:

☐ _____

☐ _____

Follow-Up Contacts:

☐ _____

☐ _____

Customer Contacts:

☐ _____

☐ _____

Builder Contacts:

☐ _____

☐ _____

Gratitude:

☐ _____

NOVEMBER 4TH

☐ Supplements   ☐ Water   ☐ Meditate/Mindset   ☐ Movement

To Do List:

☐ _____

☐ _____

☐ _____

☐ _____

☐ _____

New Prospect Contacts:

☐ _____

☐ _____

Follow-Up Contacts:

☐ _____

☐ _____

Customer Contacts:

☐ _____

☐ _____

Builder Contacts:

☐ _____

☐ _____

Gratitude:

☐ _____

NOVEMBER 5TH

☐ Supplements   ☐ Water   ☐ Meditate/Mindset   ☐ Movement

To Do List:

☐ _____

☐ _____

☐ _____

☐ _____

☐ _____

New Prospect Contacts:

☐ _____

☐ _____

Follow-Up Contacts:

☐ _____

☐ _____

Customer Contacts:

☐ _____

☐ _____

Builder Contacts:

☐ _____

☐ _____

Gratitude:

☐ _____

NOVEMBER 6TH

☐ Supplements   ☐ Water   ☐ Meditate/Mindset   ☐ Movement

To Do List:

☐ _____

☐ _____

☐ _____

☐ _____

☐ _____

New Prospect Contacts:

☐ _____

☐ _____

Follow-Up Contacts:

☐ _____

☐ _____

Customer Contacts:

☐ _____

☐ _____

Builder Contacts:

☐ _____

☐ _____

Gratitude:

☐ _____

NOVEMBER 7TH

☐ Supplements ☐ Water ☐ Meditate/Mindset ☐ Movement

To Do List:

☐ _____

☐ _____

☐ _____

☐ _____

☐ _____

New Prospect Contacts:

☐ _____

☐ _____

Follow-Up Contacts:

☐ _____

☐ _____

Customer Contacts:

☐ _____

☐ _____

Builder Contacts:

☐ _____

☐ _____

Gratitude:

☐ _____

NOVEMBER 8TH

□ Supplements   □ Water   □ Meditate/Mindset   □ Movement

To Do List:

□ _____

□ _____

□ _____

□ _____

□ _____

New Prospect Contacts:

□ _____

□ _____

Follow-Up Contacts:

□ _____

□ _____

Customer Contacts:

□ _____

□ _____

Builder Contacts:

□ _____

□ _____

Gratitude:

□ _____

NOVEMBER 9TH

☐ Supplements   ☐ Water   ☐ Meditate/Mindset   ☐ Movement

To Do List:

☐ _____

☐ _____

☐ _____

☐ _____

☐ _____

New Prospect Contacts:

☐ _____

☐ _____

Follow-Up Contacts:

☐ _____

☐ _____

Customer Contacts:

☐ _____

☐ _____

Builder Contacts:

☐ _____

☐ _____

Gratitude:

☐ _____

NOVEMBER 10TH

To Do List:

☐ _____

☐ _____

☐ _____

☐ _____

☐ _____

New Prospect Contacts:

☐ _____

☐ _____

Follow-Up Contacts:

☐ _____

☐ _____

Customer Contacts:

☐ _____

☐ _____

Builder Contacts:

☐ _____

☐ _____

Gratitude:

☐ _____

NOVEMBER 11TH

☐ Supplements   ☐ Water   ☐ Meditate/Mindset   ☐ Movement

To Do List:

☐ _____

☐ _____

☐ _____

☐ _____

☐ _____

New Prospect Contacts:

☐ _____

☐ _____

Follow-Up Contacts:

☐ _____

☐ _____

Customer Contacts:

☐ _____

☐ _____

Builder Contacts:

☐ _____

☐ _____

Gratitude:

☐ _____

NOVEMBER 12TH

To Do List:

□ _____

□ _____

□ _____

□ _____

□ _____

New Prospect Contacts:

□ _____

□ _____

Follow-Up Contacts:

□ _____

□ _____

Customer Contacts:

□ _____

□ _____

Builder Contacts:

□ _____

□ _____

Gratitude:

□ _____

NOVEMBER 13TH

To Do List:

☐ _____

☐ _____

☐ _____

☐ _____

☐ _____

New Prospect Contacts:

☐ _____

☐ _____

Follow-Up Contacts:

☐ _____

☐ _____

Customer Contacts:

☐ _____

☐ _____

Builder Contacts:

☐ _____

☐ _____

Gratitude:

☐ _____

NOVEMBER 14TH

☐ Supplements   ☐ Water   ☐ Meditate/Mindset   ☐ Movement

To Do List:

☐ _____

☐ _____

☐ _____

☐ _____

☐ _____

New Prospect Contacts:

☐ _____

☐ _____

Follow-Up Contacts:

☐ _____

☐ _____

Customer Contacts:

☐ _____

☐ _____

Builder Contacts:

☐ _____

☐ _____

Gratitude:

☐ _____

NOVEMBER 15TH

☐ Supplements   ☐ Water   ☐ Meditate/Mindset   ☐ Movement

To Do List:

☐ _____

☐ _____

☐ _____

☐ _____

☐ _____

New Prospect Contacts:

☐ _____

☐ _____

Follow-Up Contacts:

☐ _____

☐ _____

Customer Contacts:

☐ _____

☐ _____

Builder Contacts:

☐ _____

☐ _____

Gratitude:

☐ _____

NOVEMBER 16TH

☐ Supplements   ☐ Water   ☐ Meditate/Mindset   ☐ Movement

To Do List:

☐ _____

☐ _____

☐ _____

☐ _____

☐ _____

New Prospect Contacts:

☐ _____

☐ _____

Follow-Up Contacts:

☐ _____

☐ _____

Customer Contacts:

☐ _____

☐ _____

Builder Contacts:

☐ _____

☐ _____

Gratitude:

☐ _____

NOVEMBER 17ᵀᴴ

☐ Supplements   ☐ Water   ☐ Meditate/Mindset   ☐ Movement

To Do List:

☐ _____

☐ _____

☐ _____

☐ _____

☐ _____

New Prospect Contacts:

☐ _____

☐ _____

Follow-Up Contacts:

☐ _____

☐ _____

Customer Contacts:

☐ _____

☐ _____

Builder Contacts:

☐ _____

☐ _____

Gratitude:

☐ _____

NOVEMBER 18TH

☐ Supplements   ☐ Water   ☐ Meditate/Mindset   ☐ Movement

To Do List:

☐ _____

☐ _____

☐ _____

☐ _____

☐ _____

New Prospect Contacts:

☐ _____

☐ _____

Follow-Up Contacts:

☐ _____

☐ _____

Customer Contacts:

☐ _____

☐ _____

Builder Contacts:

☐ _____

☐ _____

Gratitude:

☐ _____

NOVEMBER 19TH

☐ Supplements ☐ Water ☐ Meditate/Mindset ☐ Movement

To Do List:

☐ _____

☐ _____

☐ _____

☐ _____

☐ _____

New Prospect Contacts:

☐ _____

☐ _____

Follow-Up Contacts:

☐ _____

☐ _____

Customer Contacts:

☐ _____

☐ _____

Builder Contacts:

☐ _____

☐ _____

Gratitude:

☐ _____

NOVEMBER 20TH

□ Supplements   □ Water   □ Meditate/Mindset   □ Movement

To Do List:

□ _____

□ _____

□ _____

□ _____

□ _____

New Prospect Contacts:

□ _____

□ _____

Follow-Up Contacts:

□ _____

□ _____

Customer Contacts:

□ _____

□ _____

Builder Contacts:

□ _____

□ _____

Gratitude:

□ _____

NOVEMBER 21ST

☐ Supplements   ☐ Water   ☐ Meditate/Mindset   ☐ Movement

To Do List:

☐ _____

☐ _____

☐ _____

☐ _____

☐ _____

New Prospect Contacts:

☐ _____

☐ _____

Follow-Up Contacts:

☐ _____

☐ _____

Customer Contacts:

☐ _____

☐ _____

Builder Contacts:

☐ _____

☐ _____

Gratitude:

☐ _____

NOVEMBER 22ND

☐ Supplements　　☐ Water　　☐ Meditate/Mindset　　☐ Movement

To Do List:

☐ _____

☐ _____

☐ _____

☐ _____

☐ _____

New Prospect Contacts:

☐ _____

☐ _____

Follow-Up Contacts:

☐ _____

☐ _____

Customer Contacts:

☐ _____

☐ _____

Builder Contacts:

☐ _____

☐ _____

Gratitude:

☐ _____

NOVEMBER 23RD

☐ Supplements   ☐ Water   ☐ Meditate/Mindset   ☐ Movement

To Do List:

☐ _____

☐ _____

☐ _____

☐ _____

☐ _____

New Prospect Contacts:

☐ _____

☐ _____

Follow-Up Contacts:

☐ _____

☐ _____

Customer Contacts:

☐ _____

☐ _____

Builder Contacts:

☐ _____

☐ _____

Gratitude:

☐ _____

NOVEMBER 24TH

□ Supplements   □ Water   □ Meditate/Mindset   □ Movement

To Do List:

□ _____
□ _____
□ _____
□ _____
□ _____

New Prospect Contacts:

□ _____
□ _____

Follow-Up Contacts:

□ _____
□ _____

Customer Contacts:

□ _____
□ _____

Builder Contacts:

□ _____
□ _____

Gratitude:

□ _____

NOVEMBER 25TH

□ Supplements   □ Water   □ Meditate/Mindset   □ Movement

To Do List:

□ _____
□ _____
□ _____
□ _____
□ _____

New Prospect Contacts:

□ _____
□ _____

Follow-Up Contacts:

□ _____
□ _____

Customer Contacts:

□ _____
□ _____

Builder Contacts:

□ _____
□ _____

Gratitude:

□ _____

NOVEMBER 26TH

To Do List:

☐ _____

☐ _____

☐ _____

☐ _____

☐ _____

New Prospect Contacts:

☐ _____

☐ _____

Follow-Up Contacts:

☐ _____

☐ _____

Customer Contacts:

☐ _____

☐ _____

Builder Contacts:

☐ _____

☐ _____

Gratitude:

☐ _____

NOVEMBER 27TH

☐ Supplements   ☐ Water   ☐ Meditate/Mindset   ☐ Movement

To Do List:

☐ _____

☐ _____

☐ _____

☐ _____

☐ _____

New Prospect Contacts:

☐ _____

☐ _____

Follow-Up Contacts:

☐ _____

☐ _____

Customer Contacts:

☐ _____

☐ _____

Builder Contacts:

☐ _____

☐ _____

Gratitude:

☐ _____

NOVEMBER 28TH

☐ Supplements   ☐ Water   ☐ Meditate/Mindset   ☐ Movement

To Do List:

☐ _____

☐ _____

☐ _____

☐ _____

☐ _____

New Prospect Contacts:

☐ _____

☐ _____

Follow-Up Contacts:

☐ _____

☐ _____

Customer Contacts:

☐ _____

☐ _____

Builder Contacts:

☐ _____

☐ _____

Gratitude:

☐ _____

NOVEMBER 29TH

□ Supplements   □ Water   □ Meditate/Mindset   □ Movement

To Do List:

□ _____

□ _____

□ _____

□ _____

□ _____

New Prospect Contacts:

□ _____

□ _____

Follow-Up Contacts:

□ _____

□ _____

Customer Contacts:

□ _____

□ _____

Builder Contacts:

□ _____

□ _____

Gratitude:

□ _____

NOVEMBER 30TH

□ Supplements   □ Water   □ Meditate/Mindset   □ Movement

To Do List:

□ _____
□ _____
□ _____
□ _____
□ _____

New Prospect Contacts:

□ _____
□ _____

Follow-Up Contacts:

□ _____
□ _____

Customer Contacts:

□ _____
□ _____

Builder Contacts:

□ _____
□ _____

Gratitude:

□ _____

DECEMBER

DECEMBER 1ST

☐ Supplements ☐ Water ☐ Meditate/Mindset ☐ Movement

To Do List:

☐ _____

☐ _____

☐ _____

☐ _____

☐ _____

New Prospect Contacts:

☐ _____

☐ _____

Follow-Up Contacts:

☐ _____

☐ _____

Customer Contacts:

☐ _____

☐ _____

Builder Contacts:

☐ _____

☐ _____

Gratitude:

☐ _____

DECEMBER 2ND

□ Supplements   □ Water   □ Meditate/Mindset   □ Movement

To Do List:

□ _____

□ _____

□ _____

□ _____

□ _____

New Prospect Contacts:

□ _____

□ _____

Follow-Up Contacts:

□ _____

□ _____

Customer Contacts:

□ _____

□ _____

Builder Contacts:

□ _____

□ _____

Gratitude:

□ _____

DECEMBER 3RD

☐ Supplements   ☐ Water   ☐ Meditate/Mindset   ☐ Movement

To Do List:

☐ _____

☐ _____

☐ _____

☐ _____

☐ _____

New Prospect Contacts:

☐ _____

☐ _____

Follow-Up Contacts:

☐ _____

☐ _____

Customer Contacts:

☐ _____

☐ _____

Builder Contacts:

☐ _____

☐ _____

Gratitude:

☐ _____

DECEMBER 4TH

□ Supplements   □ Water   □ Meditate/Mindset   □ Movement

To Do List:

□ _____
□ _____
□ _____
□ _____
□ _____

New Prospect Contacts:

□ _____
□ _____

Follow-Up Contacts:

□ _____
□ _____

Customer Contacts:

□ _____
□ _____

Builder Contacts:

□ _____
□ _____

Gratitude:

□ _____

DECEMBER 5TH

☐ Supplements   ☐ Water   ☐ Meditate/Mindset   ☐ Movement

To Do List:

☐ _____

☐ _____

☐ _____

☐ _____

☐ _____

New Prospect Contacts:

☐ _____

☐ _____

Follow-Up Contacts:

☐ _____

☐ _____

Customer Contacts:

☐ _____

☐ _____

Builder Contacts:

☐ _____

☐ _____

Gratitude:

☐ _____

DECEMBER 6TH

☐ Supplements   ☐ Water   ☐ Meditate/Mindset   ☐ Movement

To Do List:

☐ _____

☐ _____

☐ _____

☐ _____

☐ _____

New Prospect Contacts:

☐ _____

☐ _____

Follow-Up Contacts:

☐ _____

☐ _____

Customer Contacts:

☐ _____

☐ _____

Builder Contacts:

☐ _____

☐ _____

Gratitude:

☐ _____

DECEMBER 7TH

To Do List:

□ _____

□ _____

□ _____

□ _____

□ _____

New Prospect Contacts:

□ _____

□ _____

Follow-Up Contacts:

□ _____

□ _____

Customer Contacts:

□ _____

□ _____

Builder Contacts:

□ _____

□ _____

Gratitude:

□ _____

DECEMBER 8TH

☐ Supplements   ☐ Water   ☐ Meditate/Mindset   ☐ Movement

To Do List:

☐ _____

☐ _____

☐ _____

☐ _____

☐ _____

New Prospect Contacts:

☐ _____

☐ _____

Follow-Up Contacts:

☐ _____

☐ _____

Customer Contacts:

☐ _____

☐ _____

Builder Contacts:

☐ _____

☐ _____

Gratitude:

☐ _____

DECEMBER 9TH

□ Supplements   □ Water   □ Meditate/Mindset   □ Movement

To Do List:

□ _____

□ _____

□ _____

□ _____

□ _____

New Prospect Contacts:

□ _____

□ _____

Follow-Up Contacts:

□ _____

□ _____

Customer Contacts:

□ _____

□ _____

Builder Contacts:

□ _____

□ _____

Gratitude:

□ _____

DECEMBER 10TH

☐ Supplements   ☐ Water   ☐ Meditate/Mindset   ☐ Movement

To Do List:

☐ _____

☐ _____

☐ _____

☐ _____

☐ _____

New Prospect Contacts:

☐ _____

☐ _____

Follow-Up Contacts:

☐ _____

☐ _____

Customer Contacts:

☐ _____

☐ _____

Builder Contacts:

☐ _____

☐ _____

Gratitude:

☐ _____

DECEMBER 11TH

□ Supplements   □ Water   □ Meditate/Mindset   □ Movement

To Do List:

□ _____
□ _____
□ _____
□ _____
□ _____

New Prospect Contacts:

□ _____
□ _____

Follow-Up Contacts:

□ _____
□ _____

Customer Contacts:

□ _____
□ _____

Builder Contacts:

□ _____
□ _____

Gratitude:

□ _____

DECEMBER 12TH

☐ Supplements ☐ Water ☐ Meditate/Mindset ☐ Movement

To Do List:

☐ _____

☐ _____

☐ _____

☐ _____

☐ _____

New Prospect Contacts:

☐ _____

☐ _____

Follow-Up Contacts:

☐ _____

☐ _____

Customer Contacts:

☐ _____

☐ _____

Builder Contacts:

☐ _____

☐ _____

Gratitude:

☐ _____

DECEMBER 13TH

☐ Supplements   ☐ Water   ☐ Meditate/Mindset   ☐ Movement

To Do List:

☐ _____

☐ _____

☐ _____

☐ _____

☐ _____

New Prospect Contacts:

☐ _____

☐ _____

Follow-Up Contacts:

☐ _____

☐ _____

Customer Contacts:

☐ _____

☐ _____

Builder Contacts:

☐ _____

☐ _____

Gratitude:

☐ _____

DECEMBER 14TH

☐ Supplements ☐ Water ☐ Meditate/Mindset ☐ Movement

To Do List:

☐ _____

☐ _____

☐ _____

☐ _____

☐ _____

New Prospect Contacts:

☐ _____

☐ _____

Follow-Up Contacts:

☐ _____

☐ _____

Customer Contacts:

☐ _____

☐ _____

Builder Contacts:

☐ _____

☐ _____

Gratitude:

☐ _____

DECEMBER 15TH

☐ Supplements ☐ Water ☐ Meditate/Mindset ☐ Movement

To Do List:

☐ _____

☐ _____

☐ _____

☐ _____

☐ _____

New Prospect Contacts:

☐ _____

☐ _____

Follow-Up Contacts:

☐ _____

☐ _____

Customer Contacts:

☐ _____

☐ _____

Builder Contacts:

☐ _____

☐ _____

Gratitude:

☐ _____

DECEMBER 16TH

☐ Supplements   ☐ Water   ☐ Meditate/Mindset   ☐ Movement

To Do List:

☐ _____

☐ _____

☐ _____

☐ _____

☐ _____

New Prospect Contacts:

☐ _____

☐ _____

Follow-Up Contacts:

☐ _____

☐ _____

Customer Contacts:

☐ _____

☐ _____

Builder Contacts:

☐ _____

☐ _____

Gratitude:

☐ _____

DECEMBER 17TH

□ Supplements   □ Water   □ Meditate/Mindset   □ Movement

To Do List:

□ _____

□ _____

□ _____

□ _____

□ _____

New Prospect Contacts:

□ _____

□ _____

Follow-Up Contacts:

□ _____

□ _____

Customer Contacts:

□ _____

□ _____

Builder Contacts:

□ _____

□ _____

Gratitude:

□ _____

DECEMBER 18TH

□ Supplements   □ Water   □ Meditate/Mindset   □ Movement

To Do List:

□ _____

□ _____

□ _____

□ _____

□ _____

New Prospect Contacts:

□ _____

□ _____

Follow-Up Contacts:

□ _____

□ _____

Customer Contacts:

□ _____

□ _____

Builder Contacts:

□ _____

□ _____

Gratitude:

□ _____

DECEMBER 19TH

☐ Supplements   ☐ Water   ☐ Meditate/Mindset   ☐ Movement

To Do List:

☐ _____
☐ _____
☐ _____
☐ _____
☐ _____

New Prospect Contacts:

☐ _____
☐ _____

Follow-Up Contacts:

☐ _____
☐ _____

Customer Contacts:

☐ _____
☐ _____

Builder Contacts:

☐ _____
☐ _____

Gratitude:

☐ _____

DECEMBER 20TH

☐ Supplements ☐ Water ☐ Meditate/Mindset ☐ Movement

To Do List:

☐ _____

☐ _____

☐ _____

☐ _____

☐ _____

New Prospect Contacts:

☐ _____

☐ _____

Follow-Up Contacts:

☐ _____

☐ _____

Customer Contacts:

☐ _____

☐ _____

Builder Contacts:

☐ _____

☐ _____

Gratitude:

☐ _____

DECEMBER 21ST

☐ Supplements   ☐ Water   ☐ Meditate/Mindset   ☐ Movement

To Do List:

☐ _____

☐ _____

☐ _____

☐ _____

☐ _____

New Prospect Contacts:

☐ _____

☐ _____

Follow-Up Contacts:

☐ _____

☐ _____

Customer Contacts:

☐ _____

☐ _____

Builder Contacts:

☐ _____

☐ _____

Gratitude:

☐ _____

DECEMBER 22ND

☐ Supplements   ☐ Water   ☐ Meditate/Mindset   ☐ Movement

To Do List:

☐ _____

☐ _____

☐ _____

☐ _____

☐ _____

New Prospect Contacts:

☐ _____

☐ _____

Follow-Up Contacts:

☐ _____

☐ _____

Customer Contacts:

☐ _____

☐ _____

Builder Contacts:

☐ _____

☐ _____

Gratitude:

☐ _____

DECEMBER 23RD

□ Supplements   □ Water   □ Meditate/Mindset   □ Movement

To Do List:

□ _____

□ _____

□ _____

□ _____

□ _____

New Prospect Contacts:

□ _____

□ _____

Follow-Up Contacts:

□ _____

□ _____

Customer Contacts:

□ _____

□ _____

Builder Contacts:

□ _____

□ _____

Gratitude:

□ _____

DECEMBER 24TH

☐ Supplements   ☐ Water   ☐ Meditate/Mindset   ☐ Movement

To Do List:

☐ _____

☐ _____

☐ _____

☐ _____

☐ _____

New Prospect Contacts:

☐ _____

☐ _____

Follow-Up Contacts:

☐ _____

☐ _____

Customer Contacts:

☐ _____

☐ _____

Builder Contacts:

☐ _____

☐ _____

Gratitude:

☐ _____

DECEMBER 25TH

To Do List:

☐ _____

☐ _____

☐ _____

☐ _____

☐ _____

New Prospect Contacts:

☐ _____

☐ _____

Follow-Up Contacts:

☐ _____

☐ _____

Customer Contacts:

☐ _____

☐ _____

Builder Contacts:

☐ _____

☐ _____

Gratitude:

☐ _____

DECEMBER 26TH

☐ Supplements   ☐ Water   ☐ Meditate/Mindset   ☐ Movement

To Do List:

☐ _____

☐ _____

☐ _____

☐ _____

☐ _____

New Prospect Contacts:

☐ _____

☐ _____

Follow-Up Contacts:

☐ _____

☐ _____

Customer Contacts:

☐ _____

☐ _____

Builder Contacts:

☐ _____

☐ _____

Gratitude:

☐ _____

DECEMBER 27TH

□ Supplements   □ Water   □ Meditate/Mindset   □ Movement

To Do List:

□ _____

□ _____

□ _____

□ _____

□ _____

New Prospect Contacts:

□ _____

□ _____

Follow-Up Contacts:

□ _____

□ _____

Customer Contacts:

□ _____

□ _____

Builder Contacts:

□ _____

□ _____

Gratitude:

□ _____

DECEMBER 28TH

☐ Supplements   ☐ Water   ☐ Meditate/Mindset   ☐ Movement

To Do List:

☐ _____

☐ _____

☐ _____

☐ _____

☐ _____

New Prospect Contacts:

☐ _____

☐ _____

Follow-Up Contacts:

☐ _____

☐ _____

Customer Contacts:

☐ _____

☐ _____

Builder Contacts:

☐ _____

☐ _____

Gratitude:

☐ _____

DECEMBER 29TH

☐ Supplements   ☐ Water   ☐ Meditate/Mindset   ☐ Movement

To Do List:

☐ _____

☐ _____

☐ _____

☐ _____

☐ _____

New Prospect Contacts:

☐ _____

☐ _____

Follow-Up Contacts:

☐ _____

☐ _____

Customer Contacts:

☐ _____

☐ _____

Builder Contacts:

☐ _____

☐ _____

Gratitude:

☐ _____

DECEMBER 30TH

To Do List:

- [ ] _____
- [ ] _____
- [ ] _____
- [ ] _____
- [ ] _____

New Prospect Contacts:

- [ ] _____
- [ ] _____

Follow-Up Contacts:

- [ ] _____
- [ ] _____

Customer Contacts:

- [ ] _____
- [ ] _____

Builder Contacts:

- [ ] _____
- [ ] _____

Gratitude:

- [ ] _____

DECEMBER 31ST

To Do List:

☐ _____

☐ _____

☐ _____

☐ _____

☐ _____

New Prospect Contacts:

☐ _____

☐ _____

Follow-Up Contacts:

☐ _____

☐ _____

Customer Contacts:

☐ _____

☐ _____

Builder Contacts:

☐ _____

☐ _____

Gratitude:

☐ _____

Made in the USA
Lexington, KY
12 April 2019